The Art of Warli Painting

Beginners guide to Warli Paintings

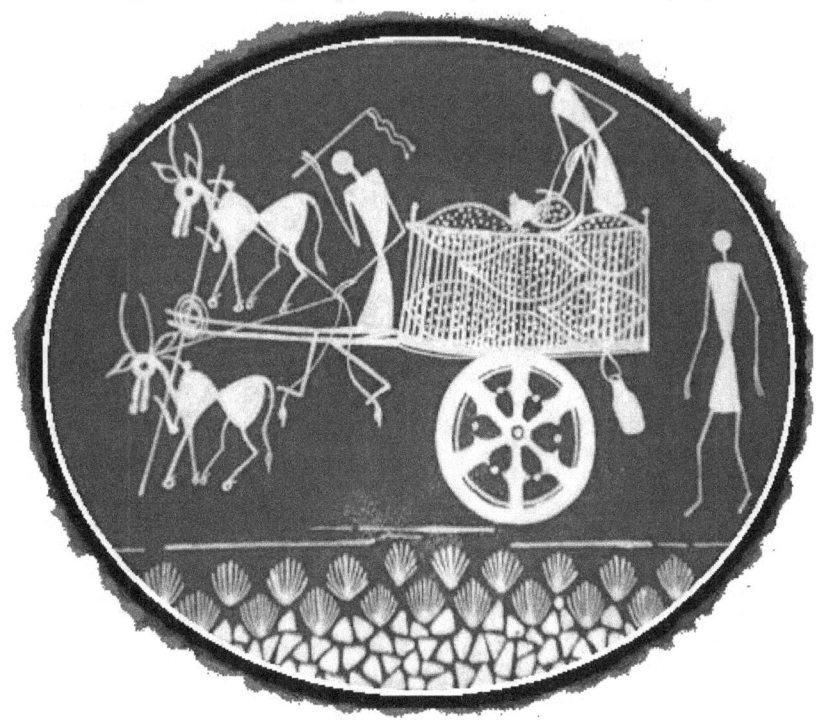

- Santosh Mali -

Disclaimer

All the material contained in this book is provided for educational and informational purposes only. No responsibility can be taken for any results or outcomes resulting from the use of this material.

While every attempt has been made to provide information that is both accurate and effective, the author does not assume any responsibility for the accuracy or use/misuse of this information.

Table of Contents

Preface
Chapter 1: Who Are the Warli?
Chapter 2: The Art of Drawing Human Characters
Chapter 3: The Art of Drawing Animal characters
Chapter 4: The Art of Drawing Birds in Warli Painting
Chapter 5: The Art of Drawing Trees in Warli Paintings
Chapter 6: Tribal Dances in Warli Painting
Chapter 7: Various Themes of Warli Paintings
Thanking You!

Preface

Welcome!

Thank you so much for buying "The Art of Warli Painting" and for showing your kind interest in traditional and cultural painting- known as Warli Paintings. I know you will find it to be full of great value.

In exchange for your purchase I am going to reveal to you some of the best ways you can draw the Warli painting. If you are a complete beginner who doesn't know how to draw Warli painting or if you know already, this guide will help you to draw best Warli painting than other.

I have seen many Warli paintings over the internet and many galleries. But the characters drawn in those paintings, was not acceptable to me and I guess you too.

As belong from the Warli community, besides to my education, my interest and observations of cultural and social life of my community Warli painting became my favorite hobby.

This facts show me the way to write "The Art of Warli Painting".

I stand behind these methods 100% and I am very excited to share it with you because I know it will make your work very well for you.

I will not fill up this book with a bunch of fluff. What you will get is only actionable steps that I personally follow.

Once you are done reading this book from start to finish, I have no doubt in my mind that you will know for sure that these tips and tricks help you making your own unique and beautiful Warli painting, if you are not interested to buying them elsewhere.

You will find the real paintings created by Rajesh Dhangada, my cousin for supporting my view. You can observe it, refer it along way.

Alright friends, the way to get started is to quit talking and begin doing.

So, let's get started right now!

Chapter 1: Who Are the Warli?

In the age of Ashmayug (Stone Era), the southern region of the Gujarat and the north region of Maharashtra were known as "Warlaat".

The people in this region were doing farm in the forest area for their living.

Before the beginning of the monsoon season, they were collecting the dry wastage of trees and spread over cattle dung on land and finally they burnt it. This process was known as "Waral", and the people who were making this Waral called as 'Warli".

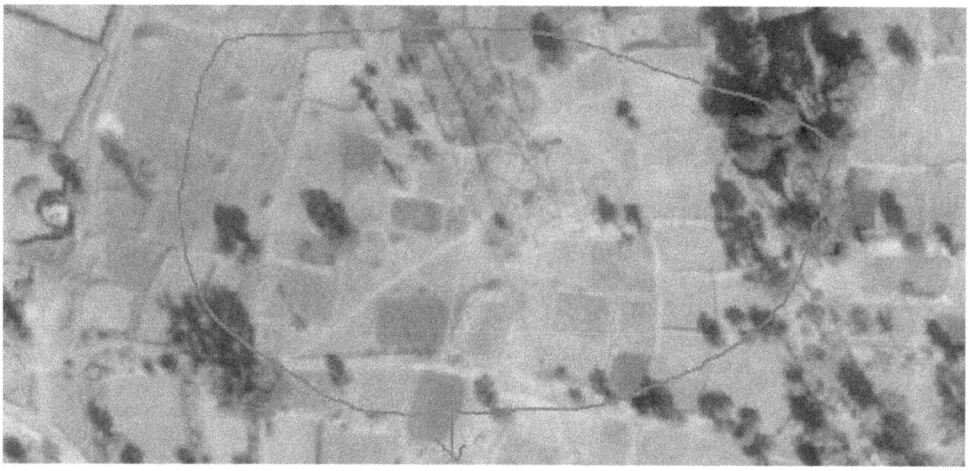

These people were illiterate and may be the painting is one of way to express their feeling and recall memories where they went.

Later on, this form of painting was promoted as "Warli Painting" and now days this painting is populated and becoming famous in various countries in the world.

Basically, the word "Warli" is a group of tribal people who mostly lived in north region of Maharashtra. Though this painting is commonly known as Warli Painting, it is also known as "Traditional Painting".

Warli painting is the basis and shows the value of tribal culture. This painting, basically; done on social, spiritual and geographical culture of Warli community.

So when it is done, each and every page of Warli painting interprets the history of Warli community.

Warli painting is simpler than any other form of paintings, if you are familiar with their culture and life styles.

Every human being is depends on nature and Warli painting is the part of nature. It teaches us to love on nature, it teaches us to live in community, it teaches us to work in unity and politely...

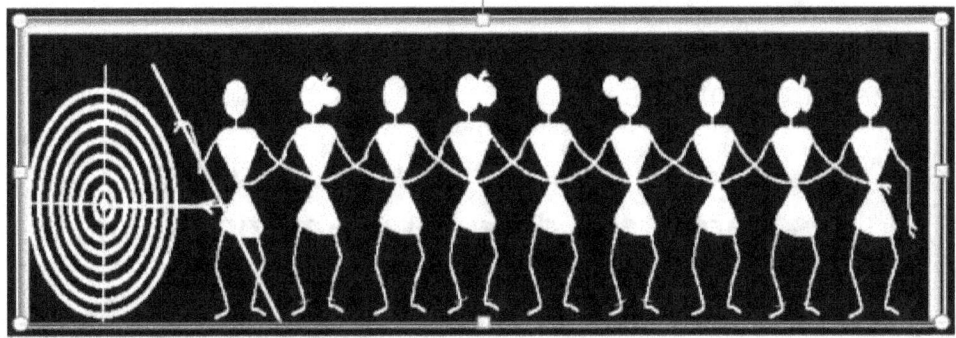

Let's start our actual work...

Chapter 2: The Art of Drawing Human Characters

Almost in all the Warli painting theme, human is the integral part and you need to draw them several times in a single painting.

You may think it is a tedious work but it is not. If you learn to draw in various positions, you will have fun and excitement about your human characters.

All characters in Warli paintings are so simple. You need not to know perfect combination of colors as there is only one color to draw your character.

You need not to apply light and shade, right? So you can only concentrate on your theme to make it perfect.

Traditional Warli painting are created in two colors only, dark brown or brick red for background and white as fore-color.

You can use any combination two colors like green-white, blue-white etc in modern practice.

Old Warli painting was usually done using the exact geometrical shapes.

Here we will be using modified form of circle, triangle, square etc to draw some amazing human characters... see following examples...

Drawing Various Human Positions

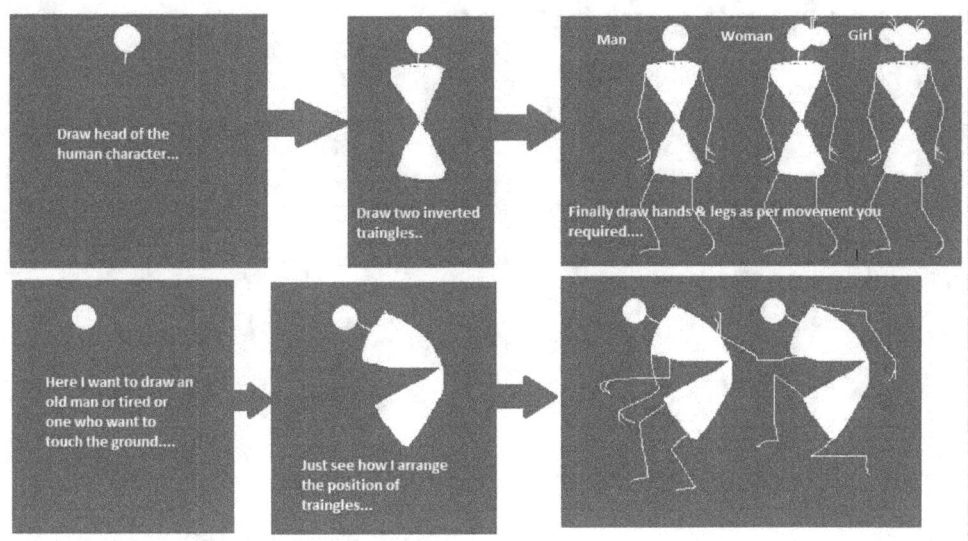

You can see the triangular shape is quite modified in middle part of human character which looks more attractive than normal triangle.

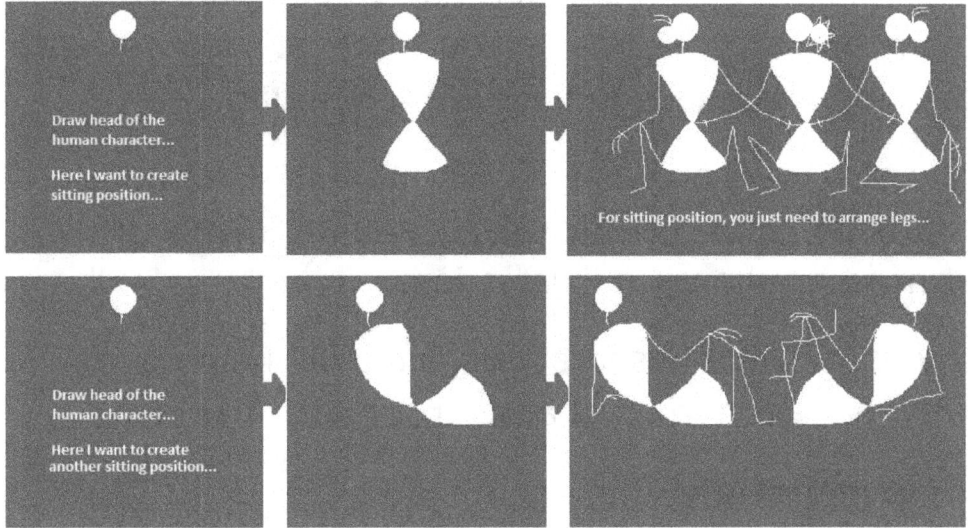

Try to draw different sitting and lying positions ...

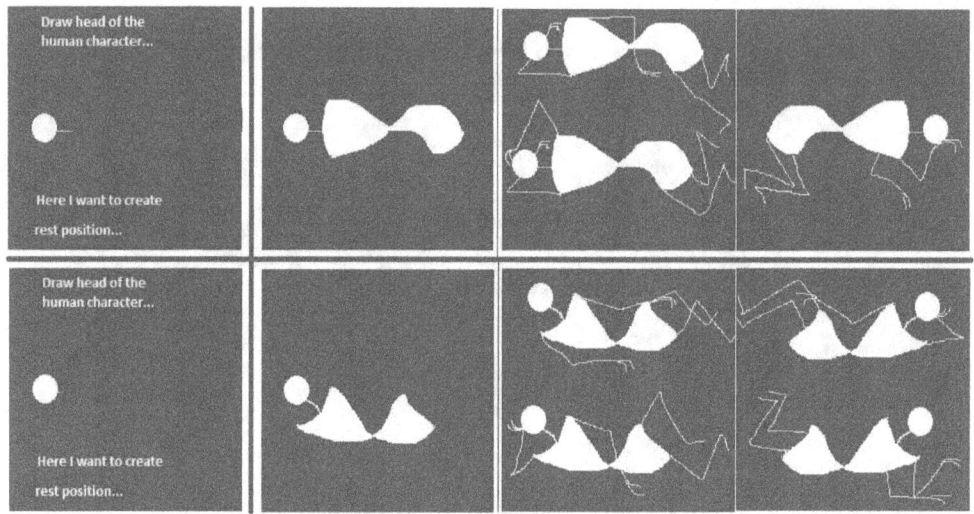

I have already told you it is simple, isn't it? Yes, definitely.

It is just playing with triangles and arranging them according to our need. Likewise you can draw as many human postures as you want for your pleasure to give uniqueness to your Warli painting.

And also you can easily differentiate the women character from men by simply adding a small circle at head as shown in illustration.

If you do some observations, that will help you to draw perfect human character for your paintings.

My suggestion:

Avoid drawing exact triangular shape as far as possible. Draw slightly round edge corner like this; it will make your character alive...

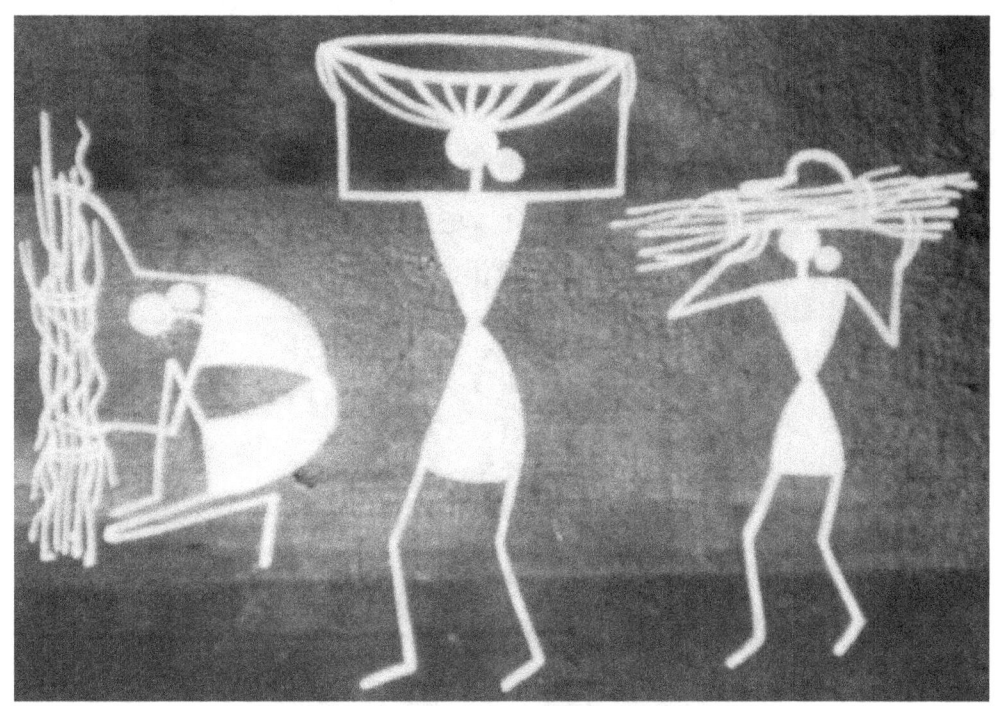

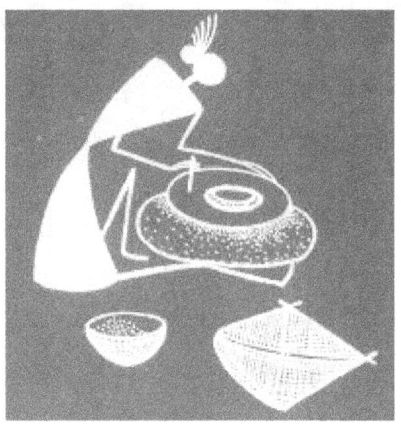

Forget about the traditional characters of Warli painting. Be modern and practice these modern characters.

In next chapters, I am going to show you some animal character commonly used in this form of painting. So see you in the next section…

I hope you have enjoyed drawing human characters in previous chapter. I don't want you to draw traditional characters like this...

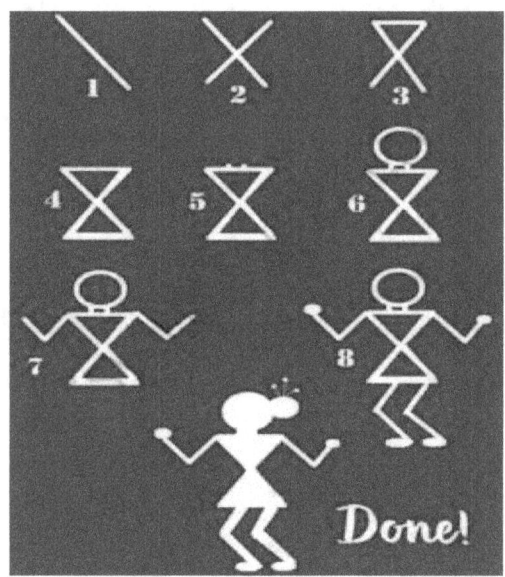

...just using straight triangle and line, make use of free hand sketch. In this chapter I will show you the art of drawing animals in Warli paintings.

Before we do it, we must know why animals have importance in this painting.

As we know all the animals were wild at the beginning and our ancestors made some of those wild animals to pets and they have used (and still using) them in their daily life. Warli take care of these pets as of family members.

Bulls, Cows, Buffalos, Dogs, Goats and Cats are some of the most useful pet animals in life of Warli.

The Art of Drawing Bulls and Cows

One day, our ancestor had discovered the wheel and Warli people have got their first vehicle known as bullock-cart. They started making use of bulls for carrying goods, in farming and harvesting purpose.

And bulls became one of the favorite pet animals of Warli. Till date in Warlaat region, you can see Warli people are using this bullock-cart to carrying goods and farming.

If you want to draw painting on daily life of Warli, you need to include all these animals in your painting.

Let's see how to draw these characters in Warli painting.

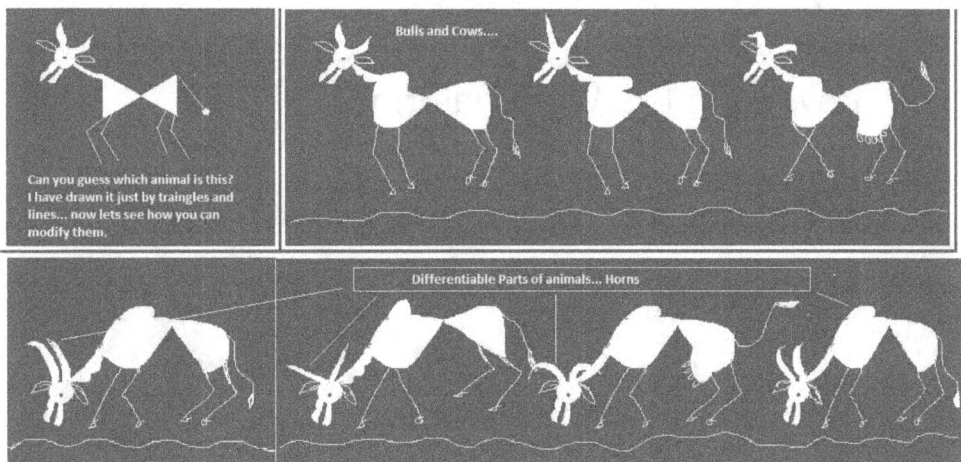

Which bull's character attracted your attention most? First that is with just simple triangles and line, or later with free hand sketching? You can differentiate every animal with their actual look. Every creature has its own identity.

Now let's see the dog.

The dog is the only security guard of Warli's assets. During a day, he goes out with his master in the forest and in the night he takes care of the house.

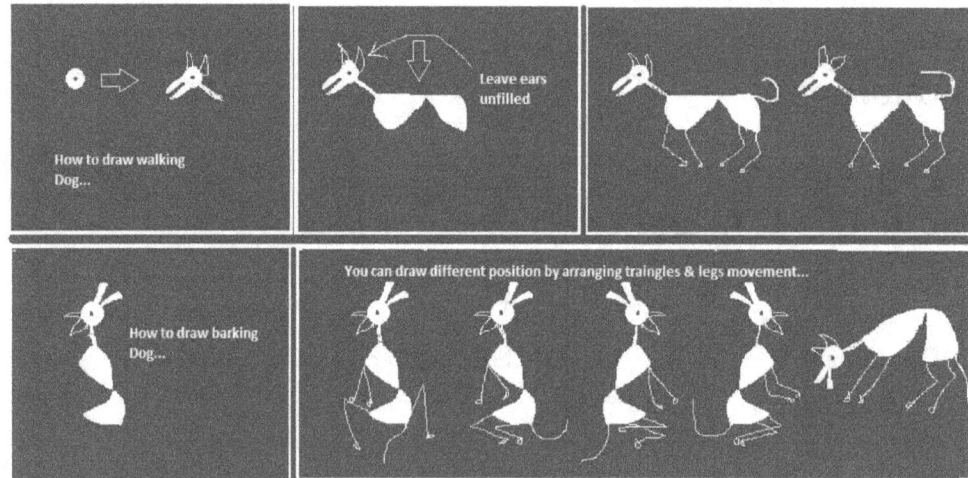

Let's see some more animal characters that you can think drawing in the Warli painting.

Warli people have cats to protect their grains and farms from rats...

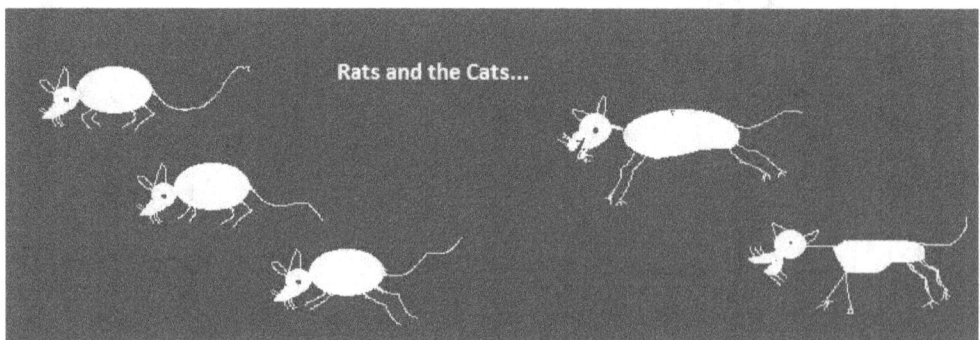

They have got some goats...

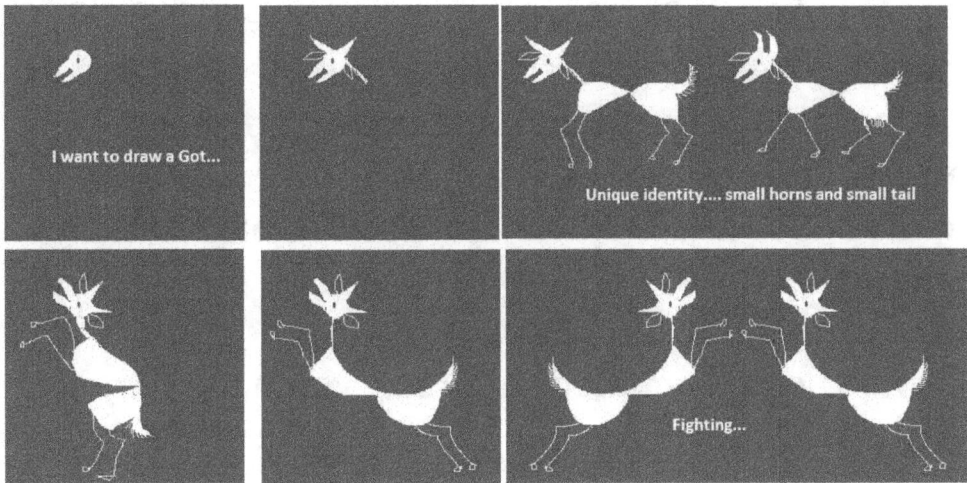

Here you may notice that body part of the animal is somewhat common that is a circle attached to the modified inverted triangles.

So, how can you distinguish each animal?

As we know that, each animal group has some unique distinguishable identity. For example,

- Bulls, cows, oxen or buffaloes have big horns in different shapes and sizes. They have long tail.

- Dogs and cats have small ears and unique tail.

- Goats have small horns and small hairy tail.

Likewise the wild animals also have unique distinguishable identity.

The Art of Drawing Wild Animals

When the Warli people are free or have any festival, they go out in the forest in a group for hunting animals. Generally, Warli live in the forest side valleys. They take their cattle to the grazing-land in the forest to serve their cattle green grass and leaves. In forest they have to face several wild animals. So, wild animals are also the part of Warli painting.

If your theme is related to forest, you need to go wild too. Let's see, how to draw them...

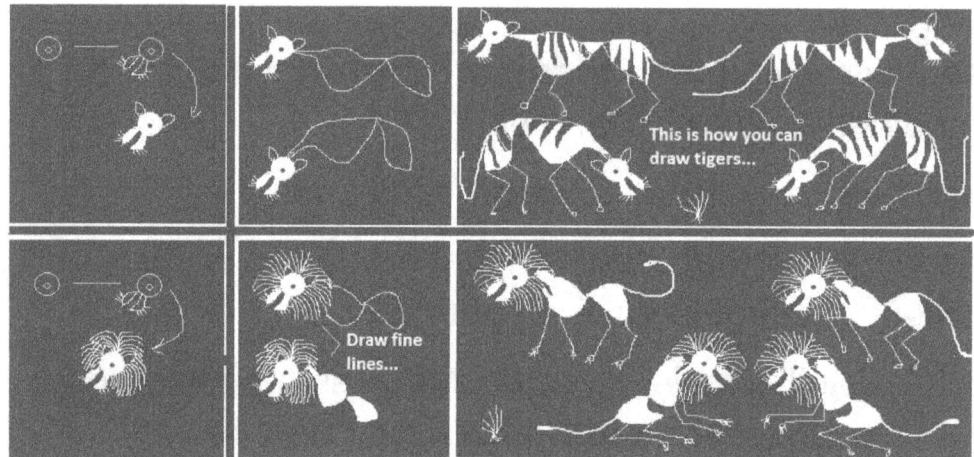

The lion is the king of forest in India, but in the forest of Warli painting tiger is the king. Warli people called him as "Waghoba".

Here you can see a tiger character and a lion. Tiger is identified by his dark strips on body and Lion is famous for his mane. These are their unique identities.

Similarly you can draw pigs and foxes in your wild life.

See friends, pigs have quite small round shape body so you need not to go for triangular shapes. You can draw elliptical circle shape as shown in picture below.

Also pigs have triangular shape head with big nose and small tail. These entire things are helpful in differentiating various animals from each other.

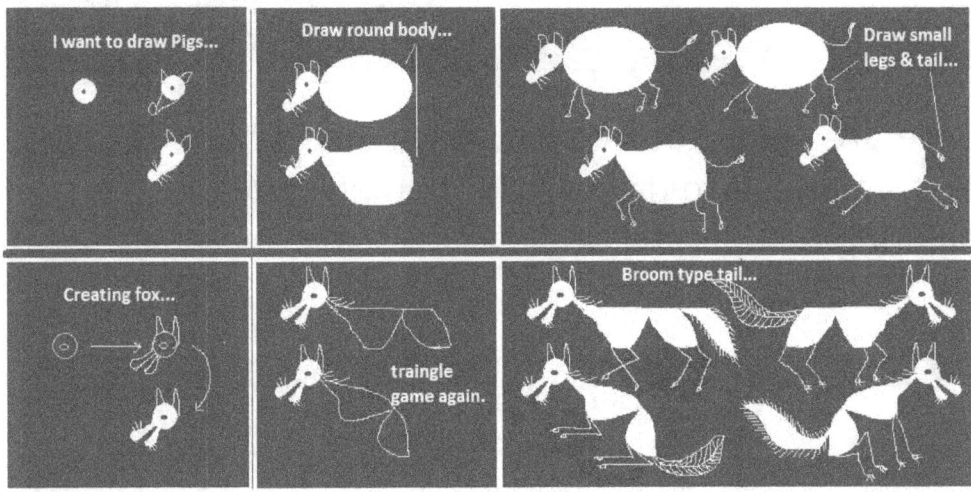

If you planning your painting on wild theme, you can forget to draw moneys and some kind of wild vegetarian animals like deer and rabbits.

Warli artist will not forget do draw at least one monkey whenever there is a tree in the painting.

Deer and rabbits are the hunted animals for Warli.

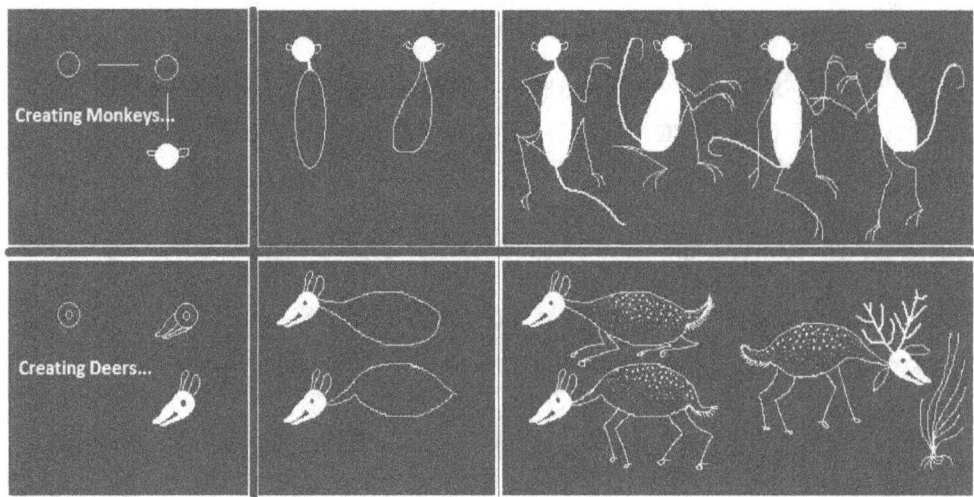

Here are some commonly drawn insects and reptiles that you need to draw in all themes of Warli paintings.

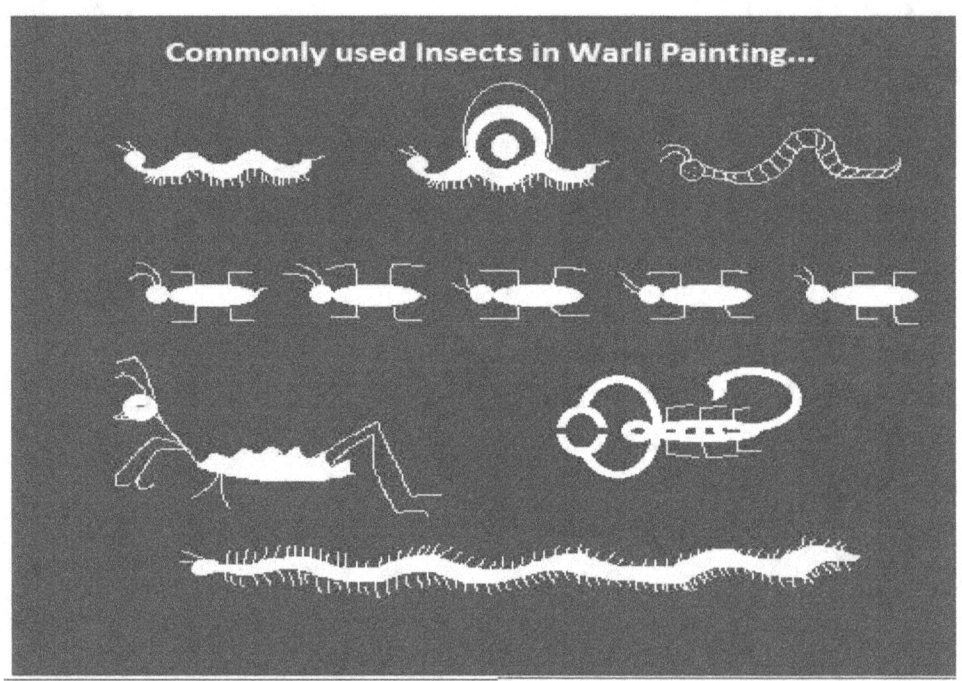

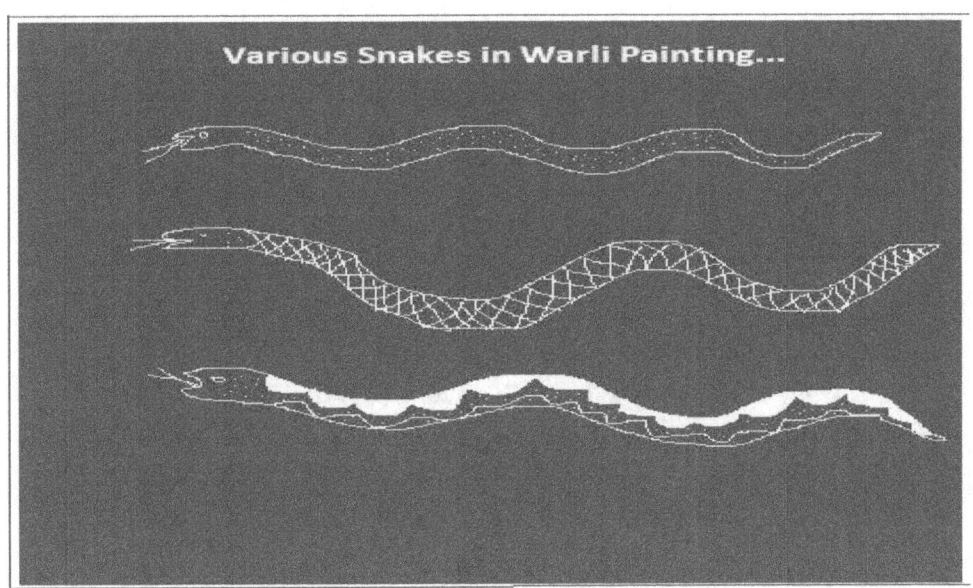

Though, in other form of paintings these insects and reptiles are negligible; in Warli paintings, these characters are important and they have their own existence in the paintings.

They are part of the universe and hence they are in Warli paintings.

Hope you enjoy practicing and drawing modern Warli painting characters. They will make your painting more interesting and different than others.

Some points to remember in Warli painting

- Warli painting is a two dimensional (2D) cave painting.
- Not a single part of any character is hidden. You have to show even the roots of trees under the ground.

- Each and every character in Warli painting is related to or has some indirect co-relation between them, though let it be a human and dog or let it be a tiny insect on the ground and a bird flying in the sky.

In the next chapter I will show you how to draw amazing birds that found everywhere in the Warli painting...

So, see you in the next chapter.

Likewise the human characters, birds are also the integral part of Warli painting. Birds in Warli painting are very simple to draw.

You can draw them flying high in the sky or sitting on the top of trees, roofs of houses and on the back of cattle.

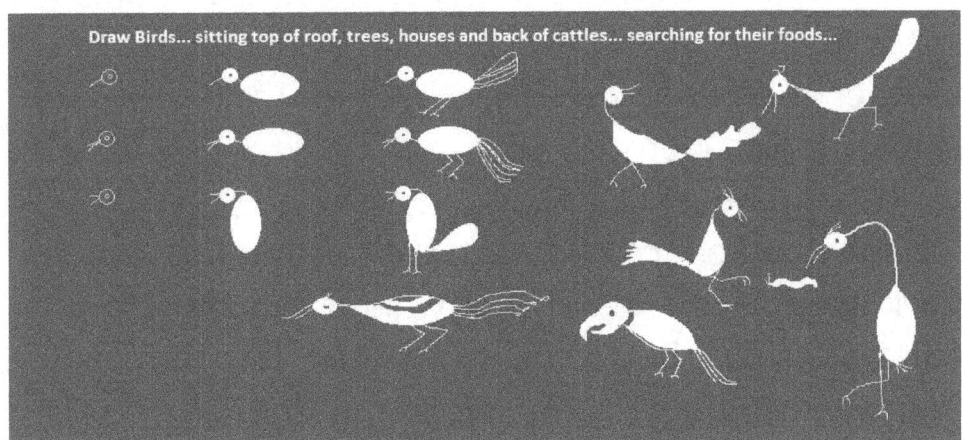

Your aim is to beautify your painting using that Warli painting characters. Here is also a designing part, I can say. Use your imagination power and think about different kind of feathers of birds that you have seen already.

Draw birds in different movements such walking, sitting and searching for foods and insects. Fly them in the sky and lot more...

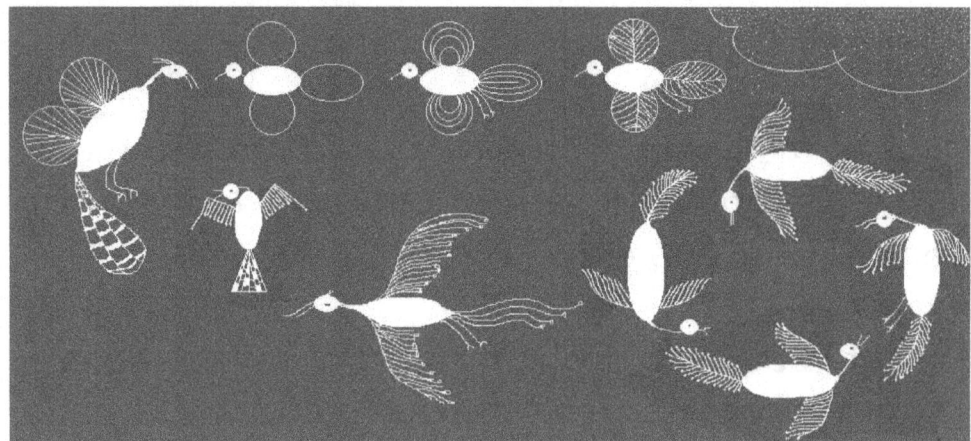

Peacock has much importance in Warli community and so in Warli painting. Today, we believe in weather conditions predicted by the observatory for arrival of monsoon.

But still now, peacock act as weather messenger for Warli people. It is belief that when the peacock starts dancing, they understood that now the monsoon will begin soon and the mother earth will provide them fresh foods and lots of grains for their family.

Let's see how to draw various peacock characters in Warli painting...

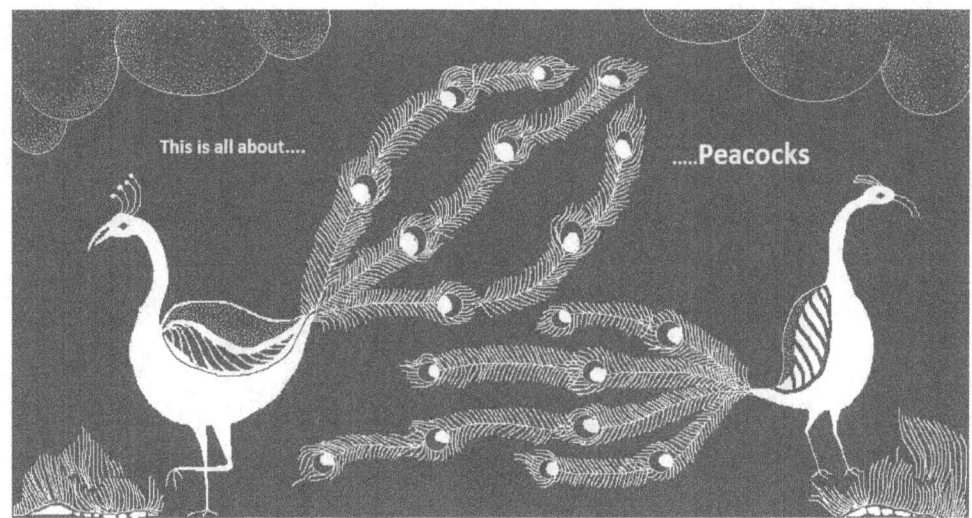

I have drawn this and all above illustrations in Windows paint program. So there are no fine lines.

Here are some more actual paintings of peacocks.

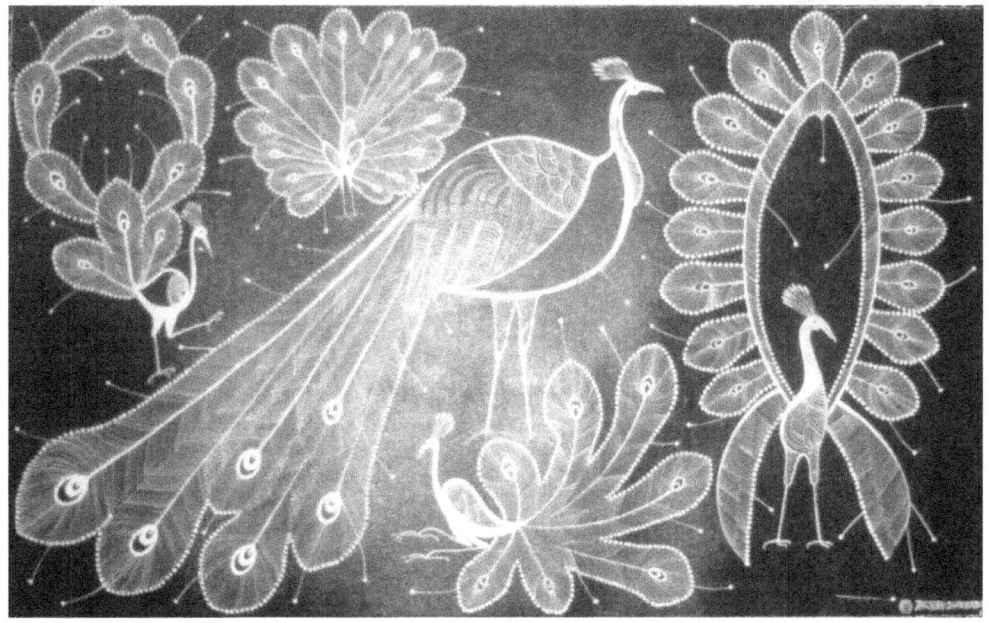

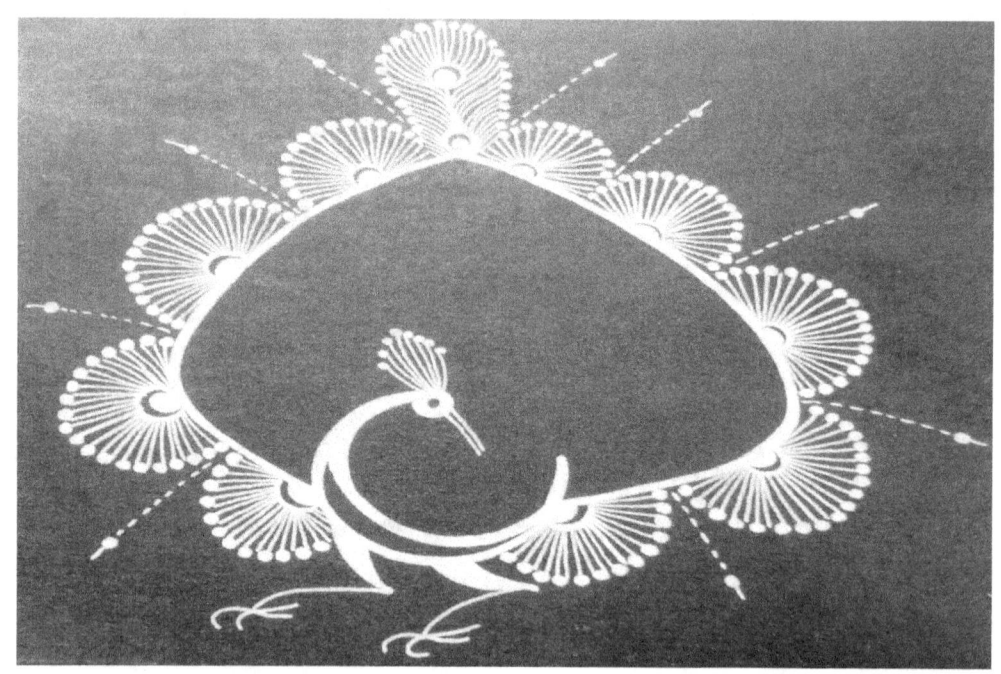

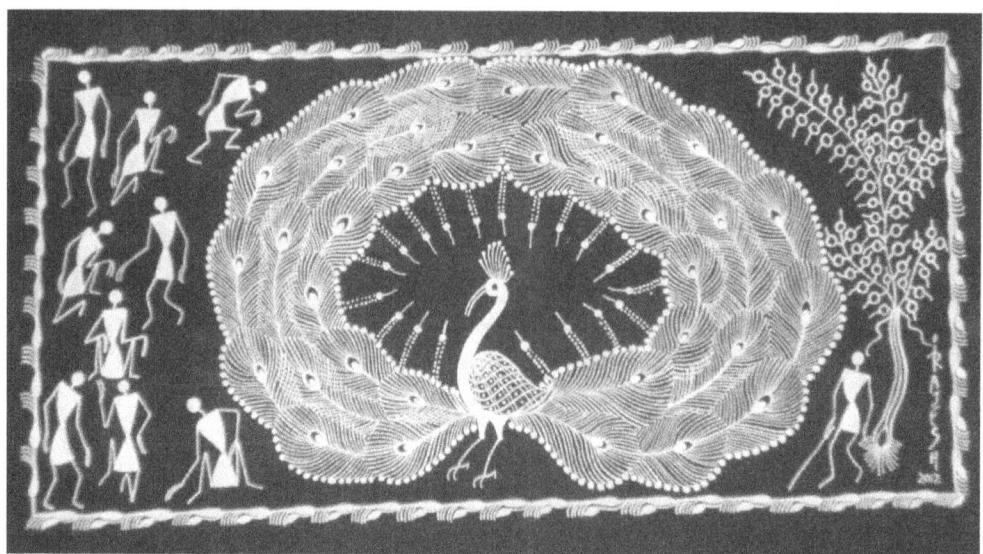

Practice makes man perfect! If you regularly practice these characters of Warli painting, you are ready to create your own painting as that of professional Warli artist can do, at this point. So keep practicing and see you in the next chapter...

Warli people are totally depends on nature. As a part of nature, trees help building them houses, trees give them sweet fruits, trees give their cattle fresh foods.

Therefore, they believe in nature and worship for providing them all these basic needs.

Generally, there is no thumb rule to draw trees in Warli painting. Also there is no any restriction that it should be drawn in this or that ways.

You are free to draw trees in Warli paintings as there are various types of trees available in the nature. I can say it is a designing part again.

Let's see some designs for your imagination...

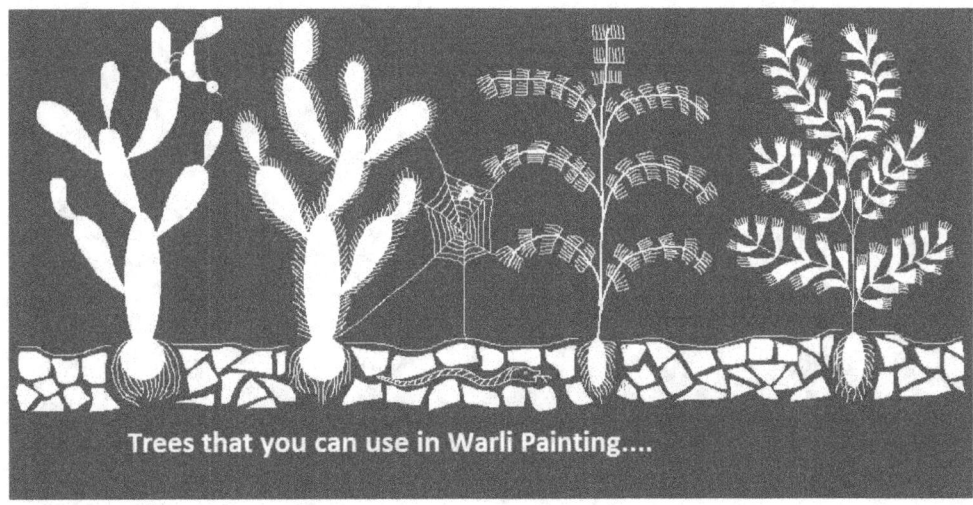

Trees that you can use in Warli Painting....

These are some kind of trees you can draw in Warli paintings. You can see here roots of trees under the ground.

Let's see some more trees...

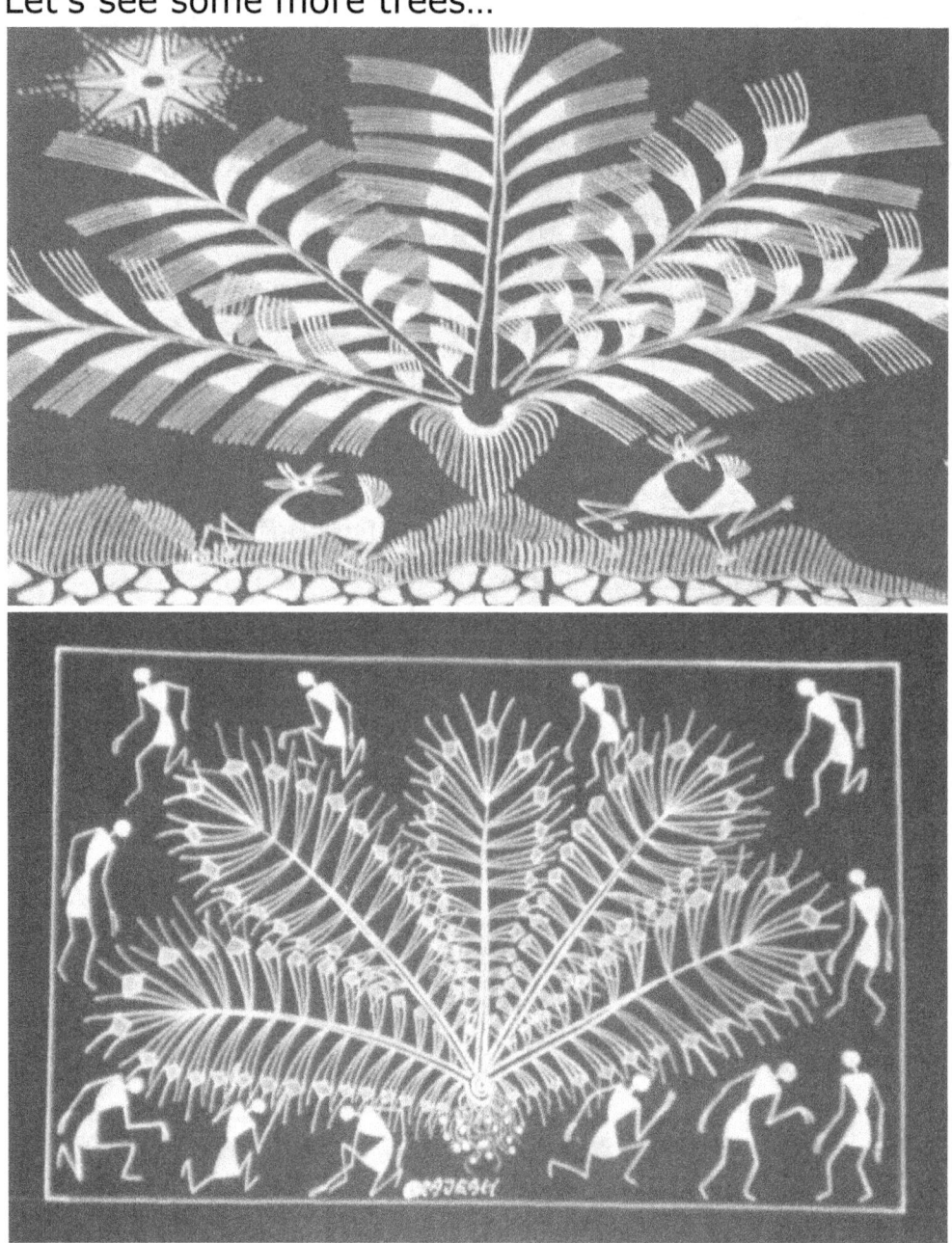

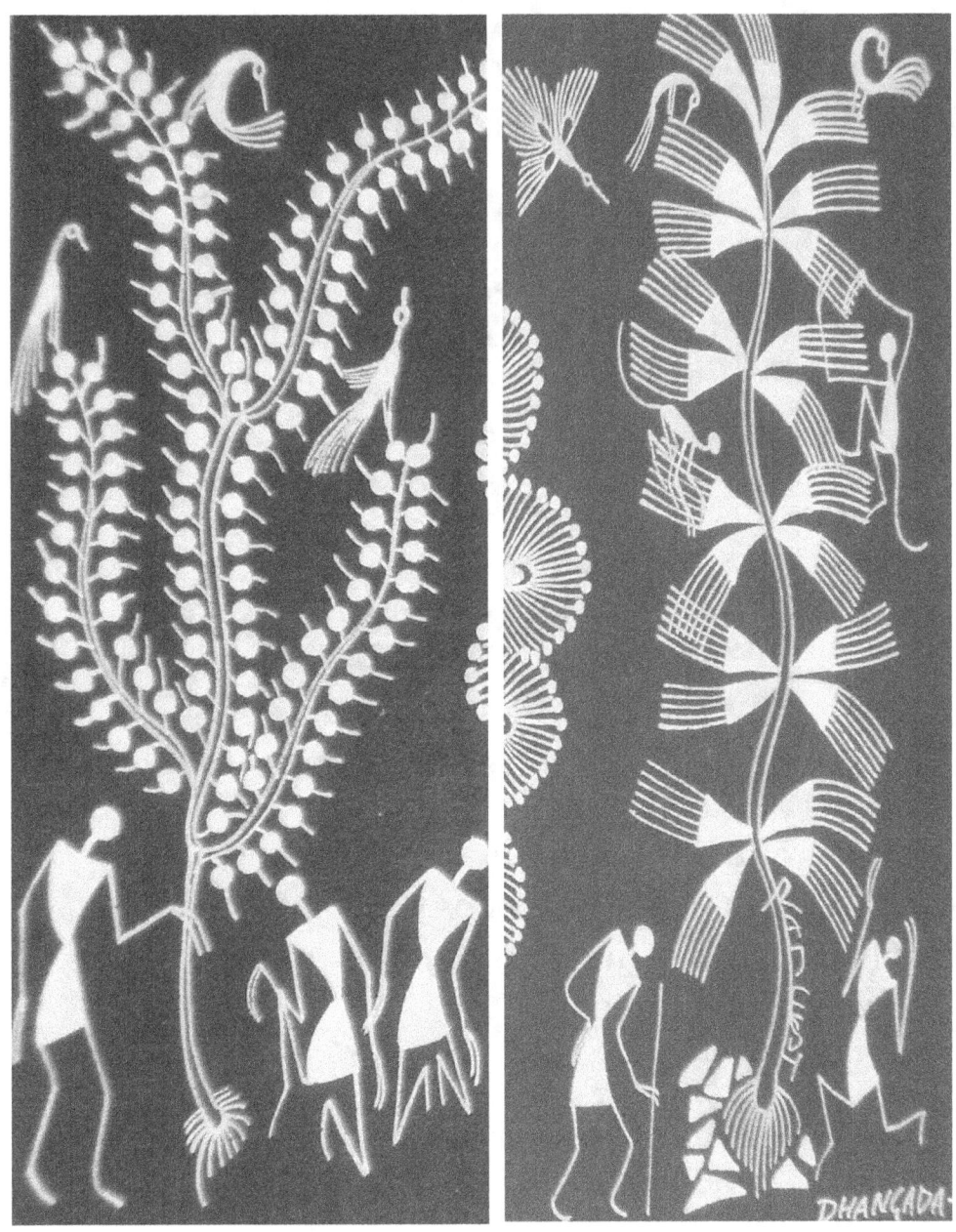

I remember that I said every tree has a monkey or a bird. You can also see some beautiful birds and monkeys sitting on trees.

You can draw big tree like this,

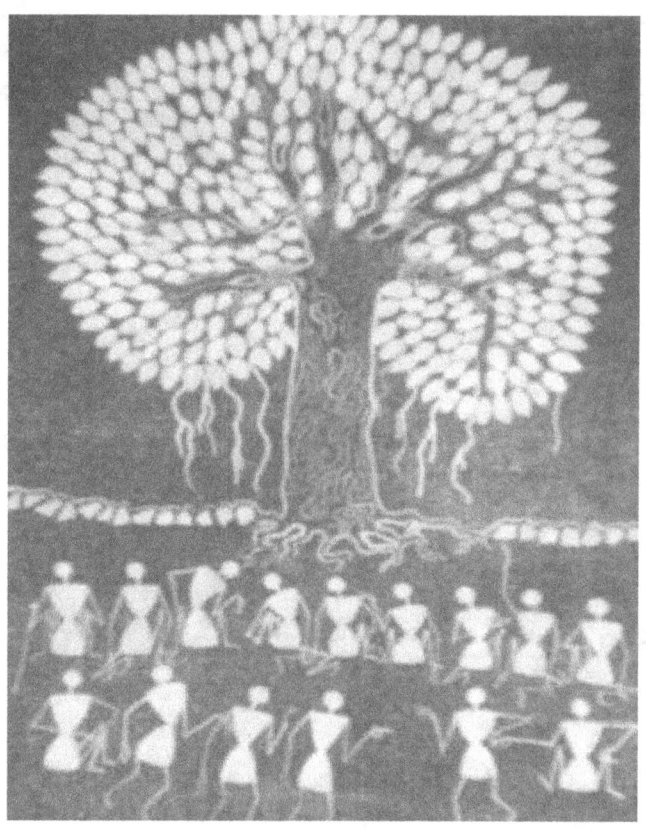

This type of tree you can draw for big trees like Mango, Neem, Pipal, Jamboo or Banian tree etc. People are always meeting together under the shadow of such trees...

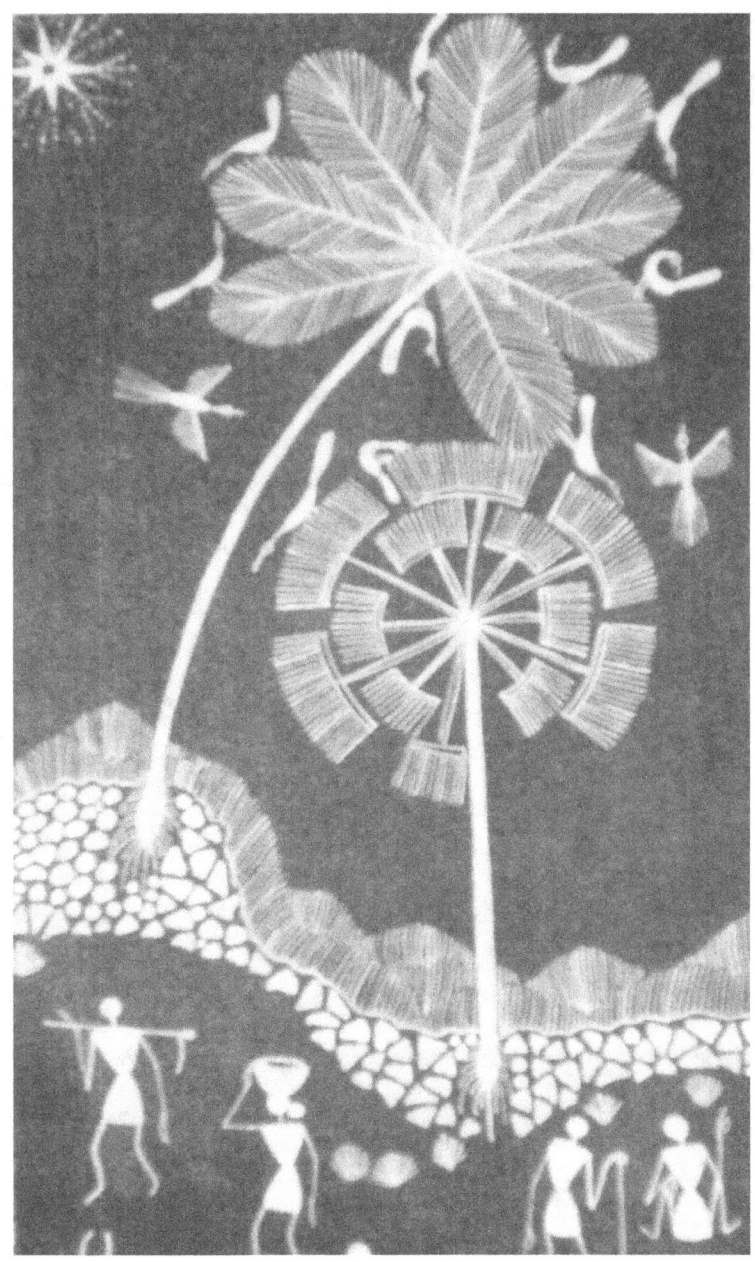

You can draw Date-palm or coconut trees, Toddy Palm like this. These are very useful trees in the life of Warli.

Some houses of Warli people:

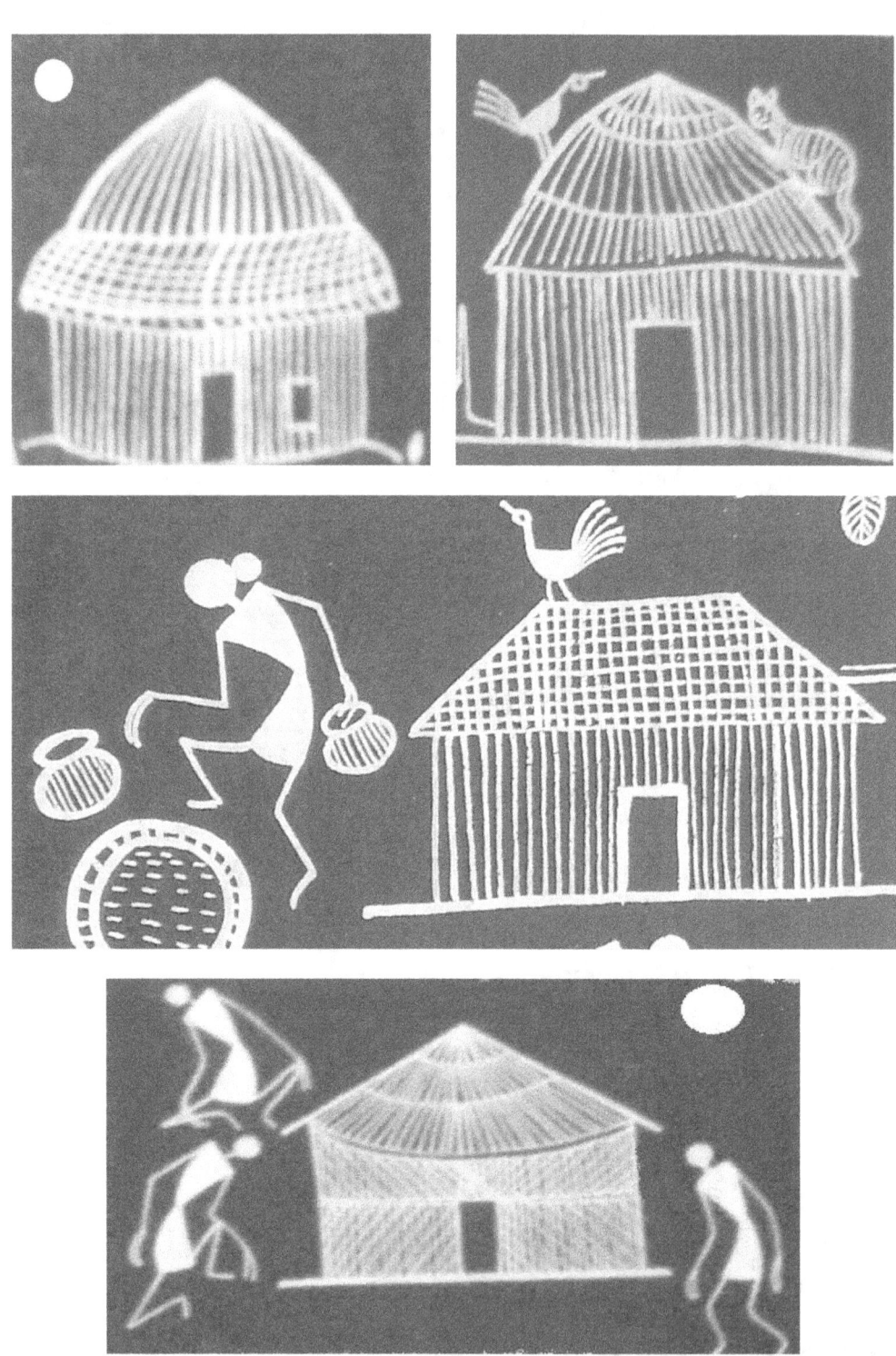

This is how you can draw some houses of Warli people. Get an idea? Design your home.

Drawing life under ground in Warli painting:

As I mentioned earlier, in Warli painting you must show the hidden parts of any characters also. For example, roots of trees, insects or reptiles under the ground and anthills etc.

Similarly you have to show the life under the water. We see that in other form of paintings you might not go under the ground or water, right?

Let's see some examples....

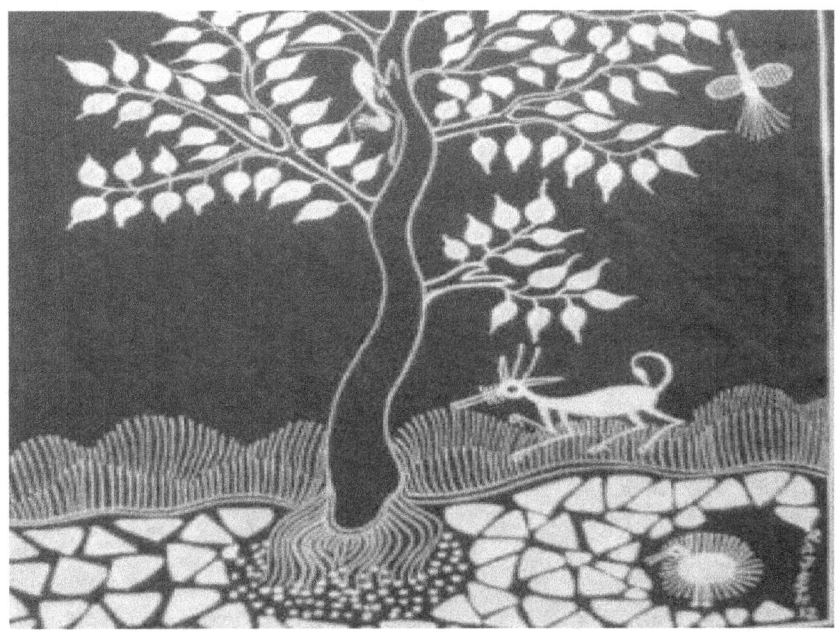

Here you can see roots of tree grown under the ground and a burrow animal.

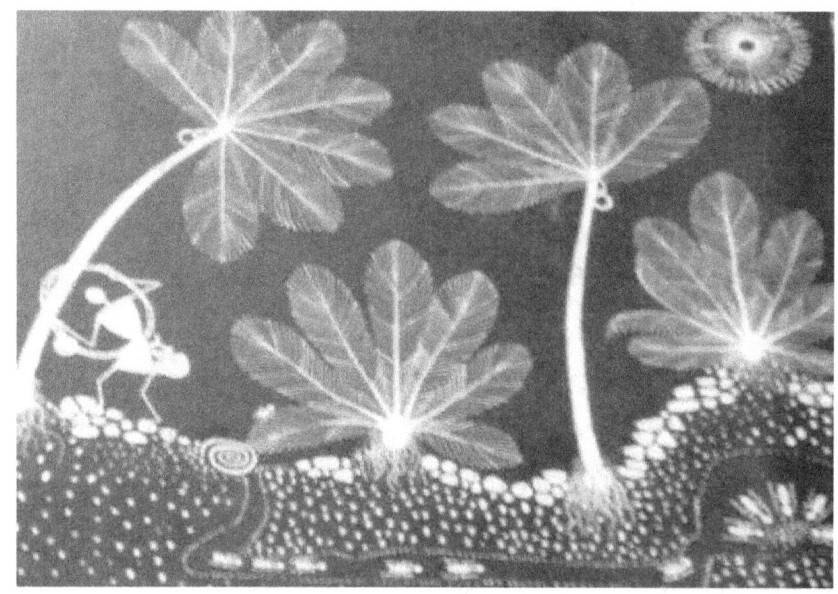

In this painting you can see an anthill and how can ants live under the ground.

Similarly, you can draw life under water. No hidden part is only the rule.

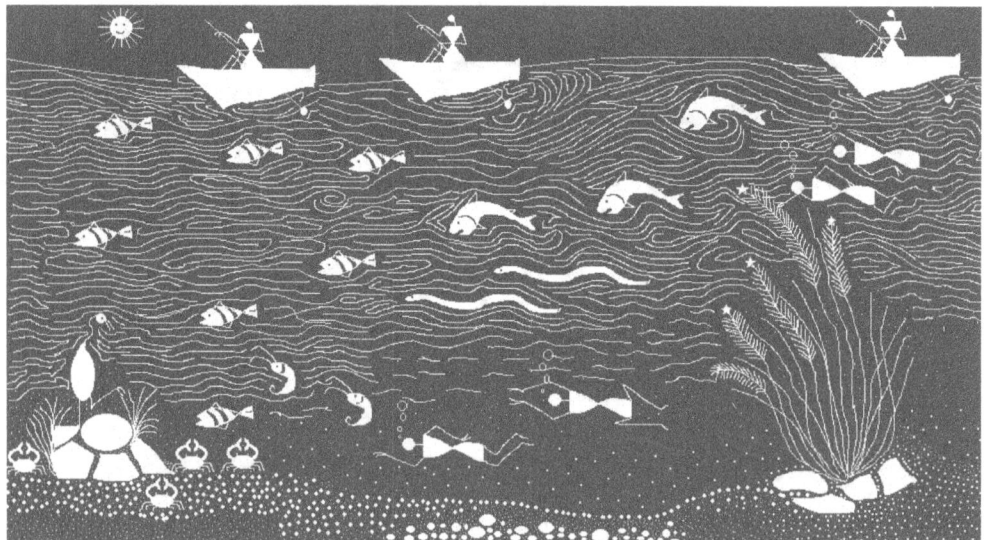

This is one simple painting that you can draw. Just imagine what is under the water...

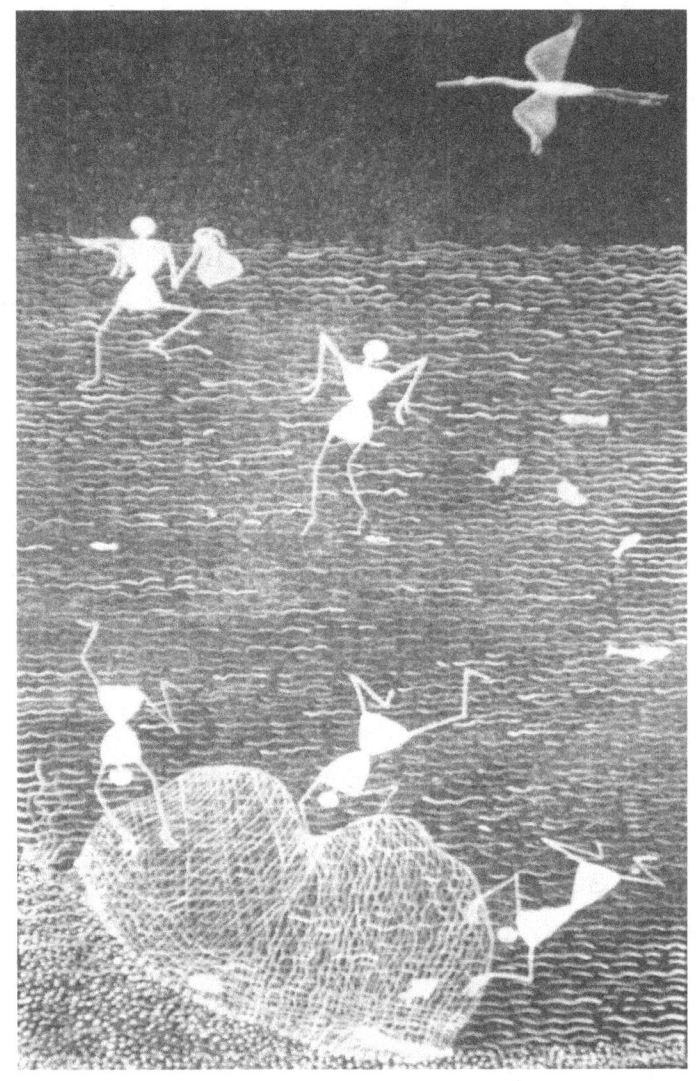

This is what you can show for fishing under the water.

So get some ideas from these paintings and do more with it.

In the next chapter I am going to talk about tribal dances.

So let's meet in the next chapter...

Chapter 6: Tribal Dances in Warli Painting

I have seen a decade ago, when Warli people came from farms tired, just after the dinner they were getting together in nearby ground and performs various dances. This was not for business purpose; it was for forgetting their worries about tomorrow and refreshing their mind to get ready for tomorrow.

There are various folk dances in Warli community but "Tarapa", "Gauri" and "Dhumasha" dance are very common.

The similarity between these dances is that all dances are performed in the circular motion and each hand is supporting each other. This represents the unity of Warli's.

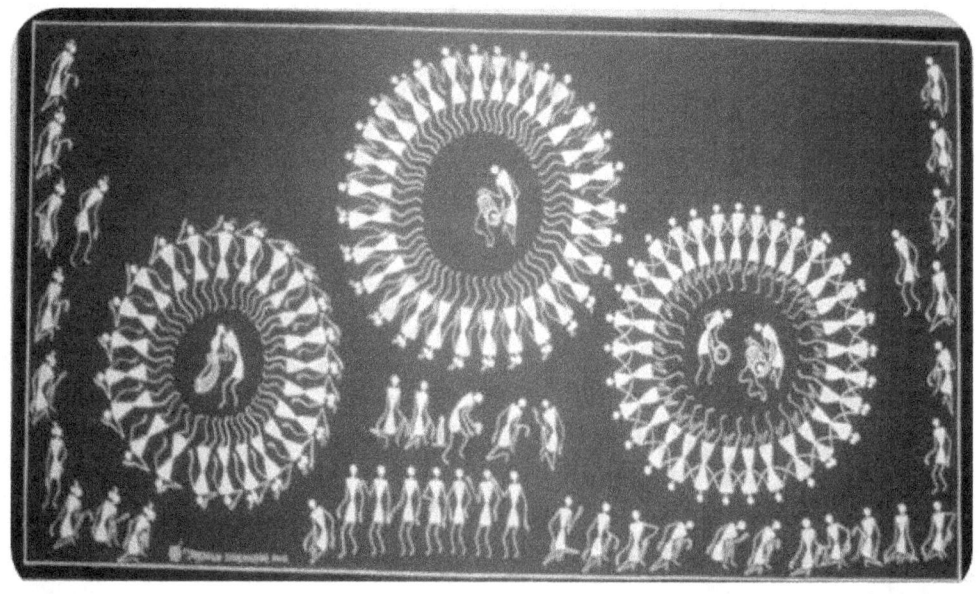

See this painting. First circle is of Tarapa dance. Middle circle for Gauri dance and last circle for is Dhumasha or Toor dance.

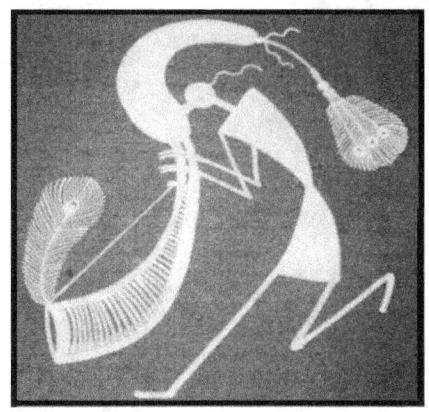

Tarapa Player

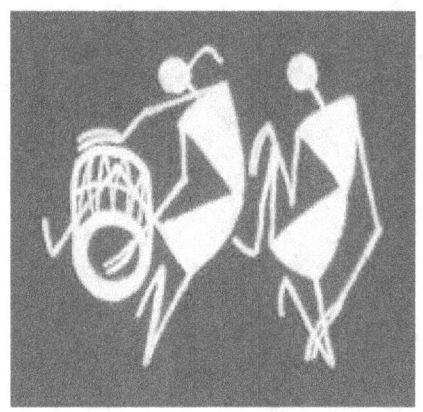

Gauri Music Player

You can't draw these tribal dances if you don't know how they are played. Here are the YouTube links to know more about these tribal dances.

1- Tarapa Dance

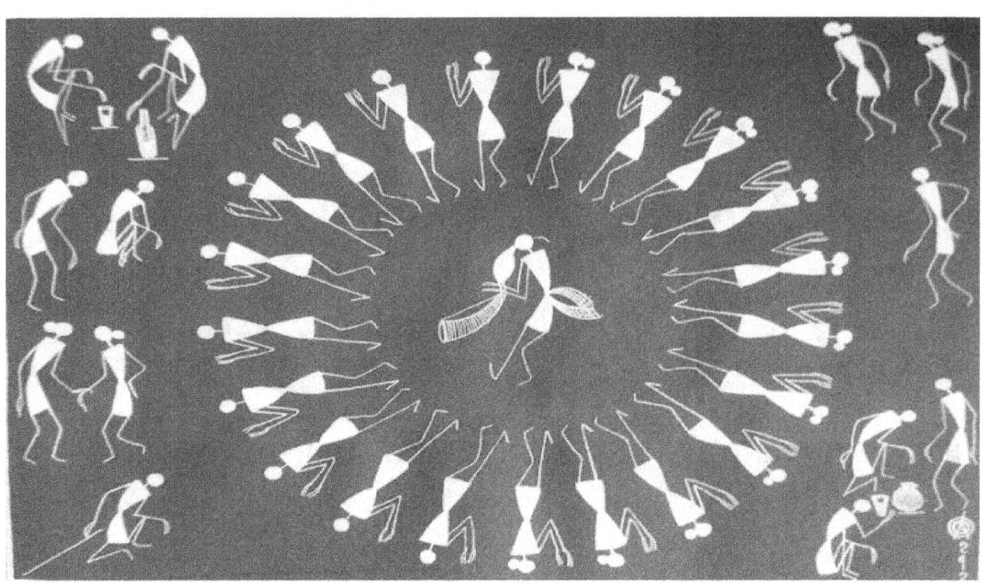

2- Gauri Dance

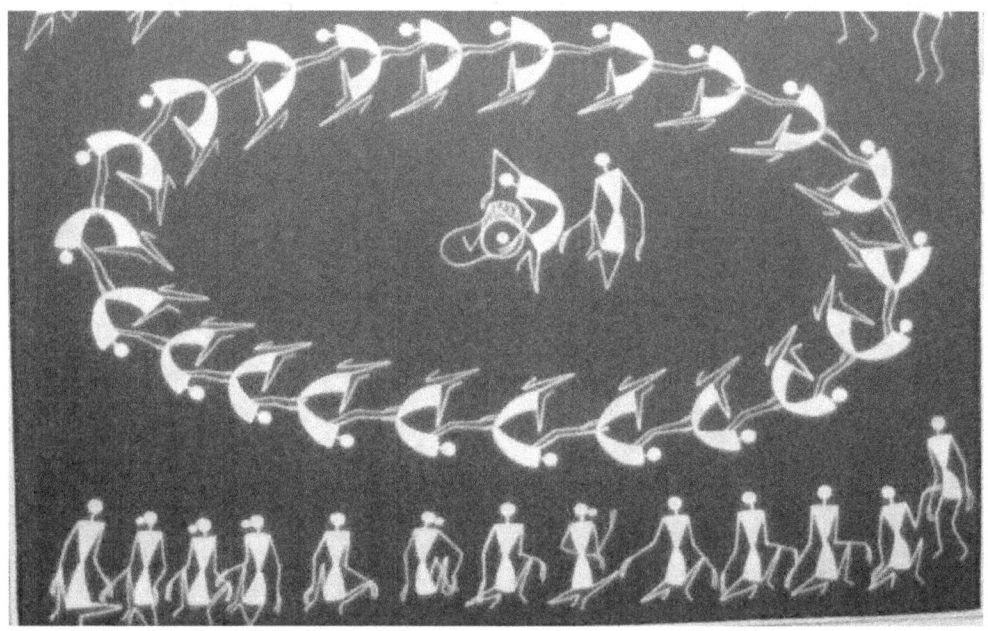

3-Toor or Dhumasha Dance

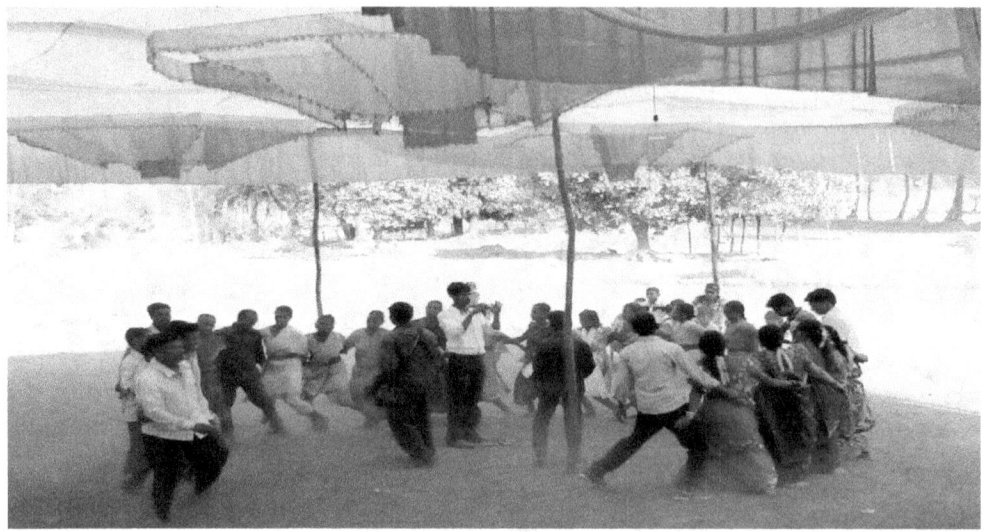

Likewise you may get many Warli paintings on the internet if you want.

But my intention here is that you draw the correct characters in your paintings not just triangles and squares.

The various characters that I have shown in this book are definitely attractive and looks great than Warli paintings I have seen over the internet and many other places.

I think I have shown you every basic character that you need for creating Warli paintings; from human to insects and from underground life to life in sky.

If you want to draw painting purely on life of Warli community, you need to know about Warli's culture, their daily life and various festivals too.

Or you can draw any scene you see in your daily routine. But keep respect for Warli characters in your paintings.

In the coming section I will show you some example theme paintings for getting some ideas from it.

Keep practicing your characters...

Alright, see you in the next section...

Chapter 7: Various Themes of Warli Paintings

We know the evolution of human being. The ancestors of Adivasi Warli were living in the caves. During this period, he learned the most of environmental changes; they accepted the Sun and the Moon as their deities. Also in this period he made many of the wild animals as their pets.

As the years gone, he came out from the caves and started to live in small huts. He formed the community.

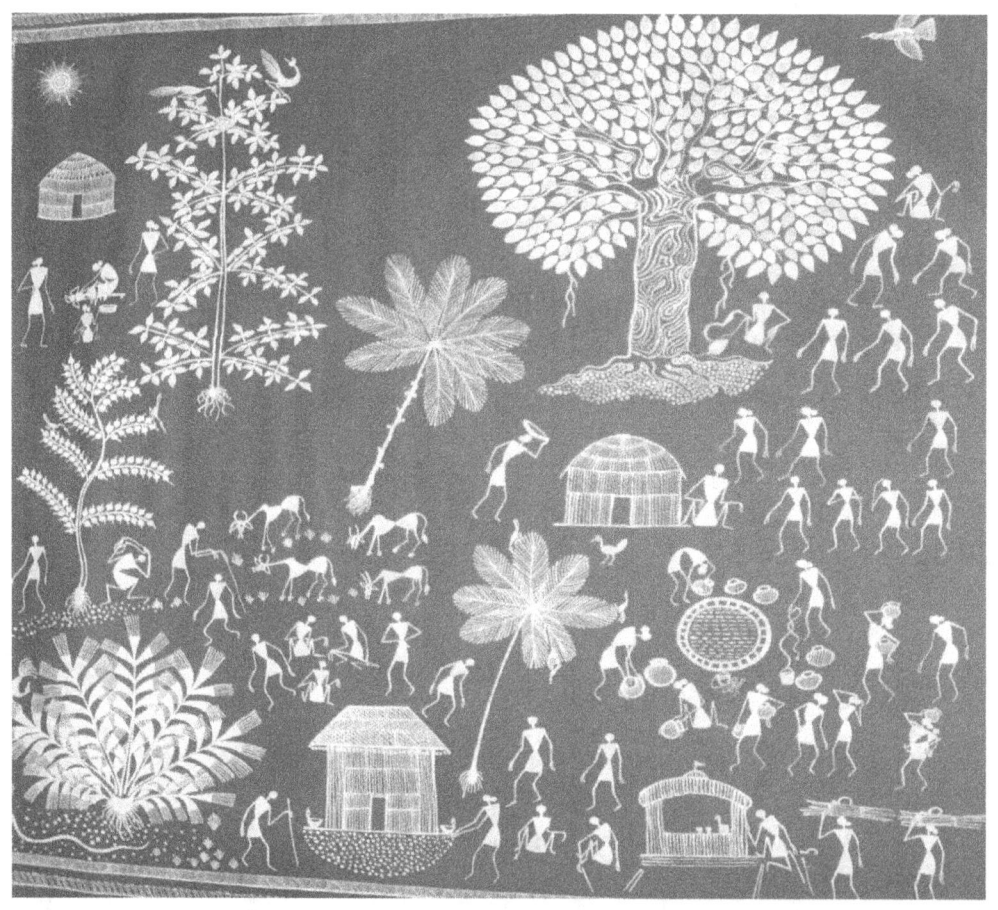

With the help of pets such as bulls, he started doing farm in the monsoon season. He was very happy with his life.

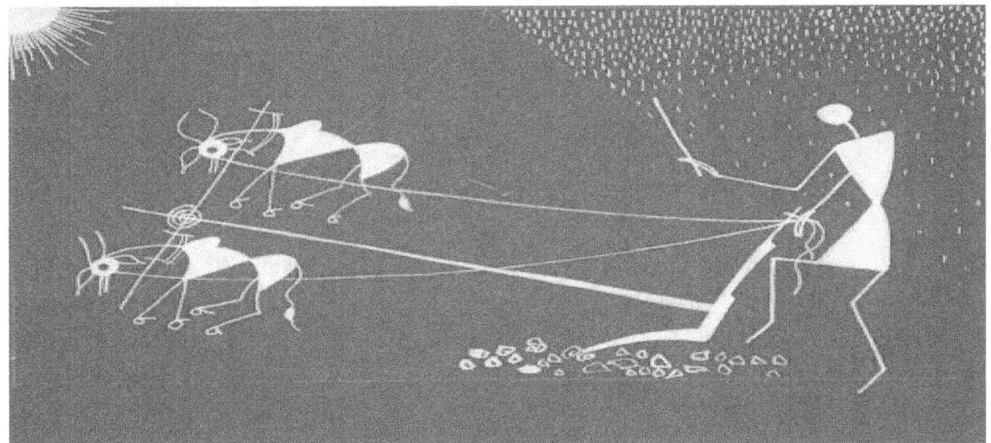

One day he discovered the bullock-kart and he started using it for travelling from one place to another and carrying heavy goods.

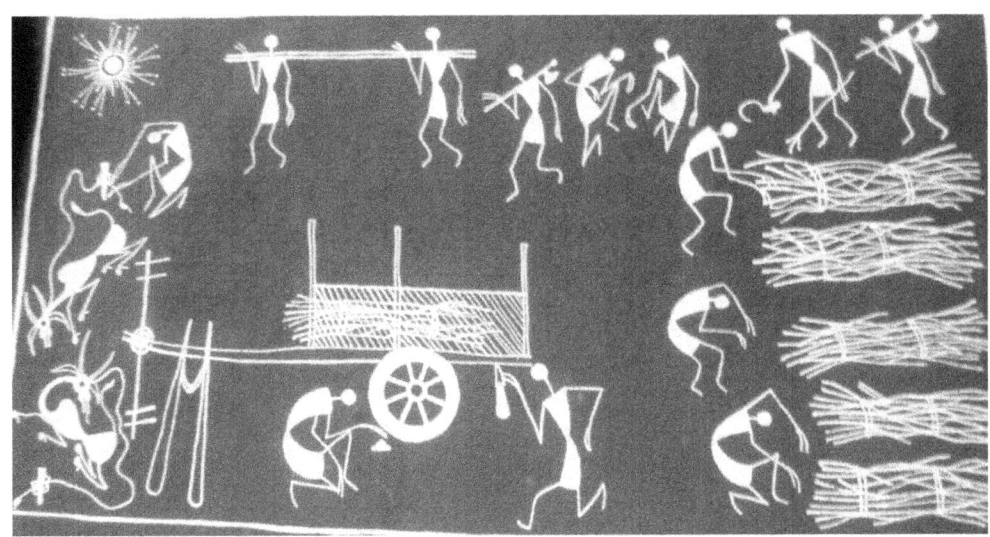

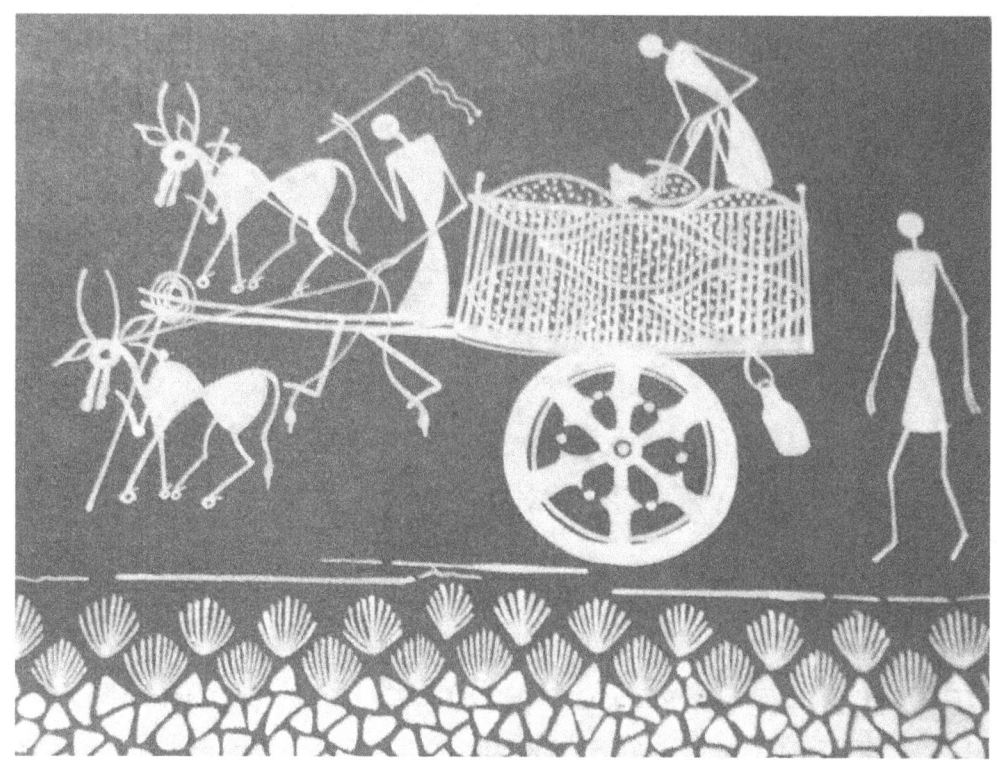

Warli woman has taken interest in all house works like cooking, decorating houses with mud and cow dung.

This was the first step towards invention of Warli Painting and Warli women has drawn first Warli painting on the wall of this hut.

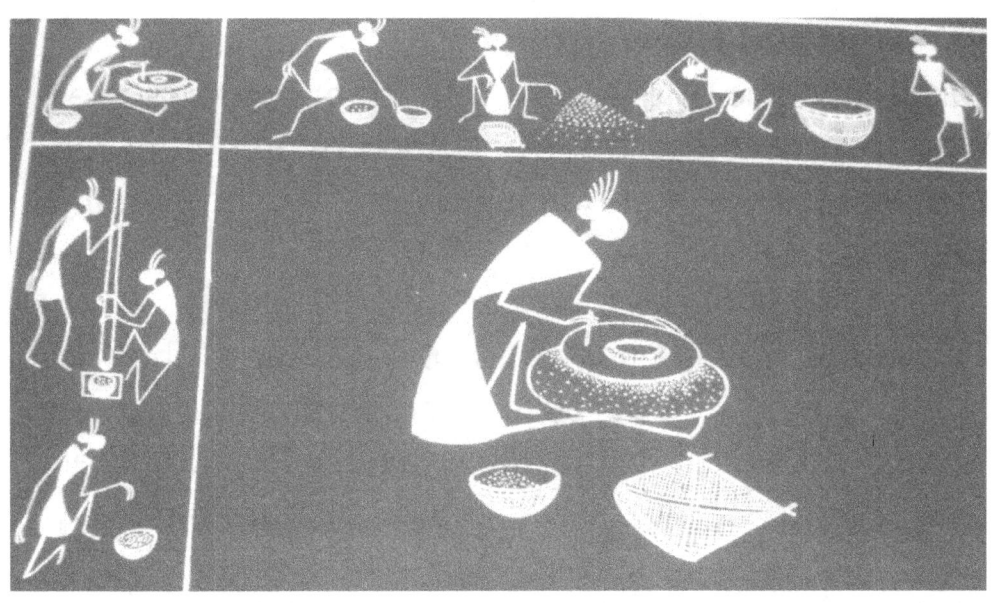

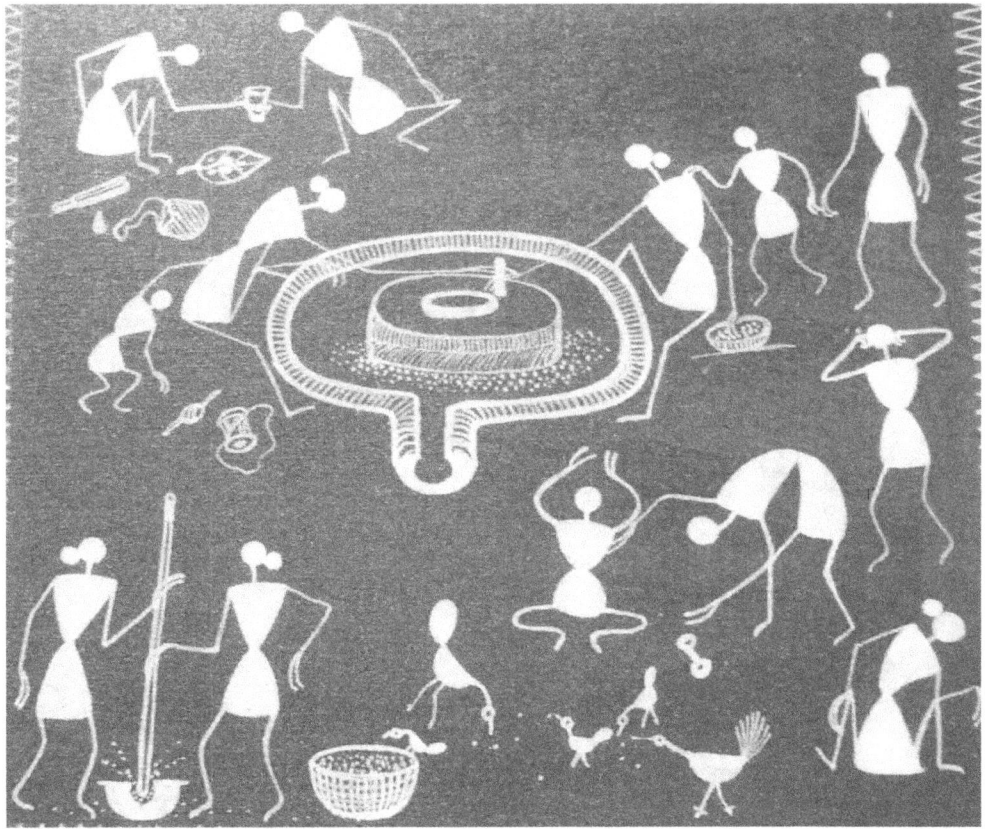

All the outdoor hard works has taken care by Warli men.

Farming and Harvesting:

Farming is one of the most important works of the Warli people. Since the whole food requirement for coming years is dependant only on farming during the monsoon.

I have told you in chapter -1 about "Waral", how it is made. It is for the purpose of bio fertilizer, as there was no such chemical fertilizer available, upon that time. And this process is going on till date naturally.

When the monsoon starts, Waral is cultivated by rice corns and some other useful seeds. When these corns grow to certain level after 25-30 days, it is dig out for plantation in paddy field.

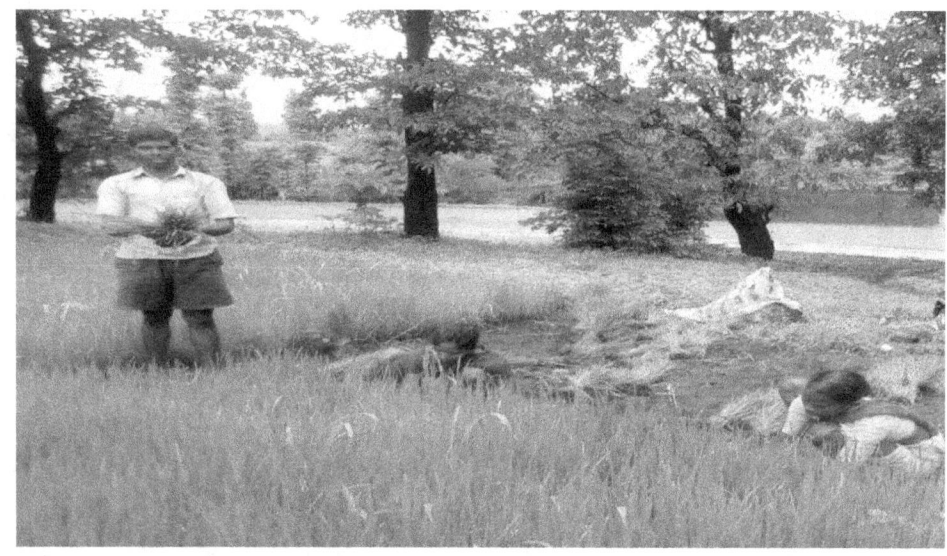

Digging out rice from Waral

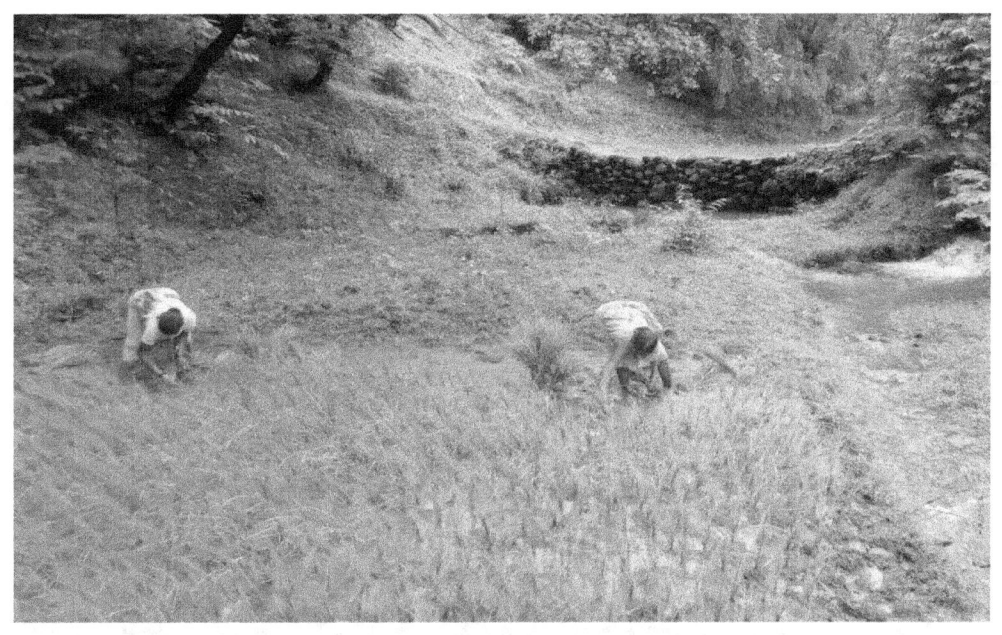

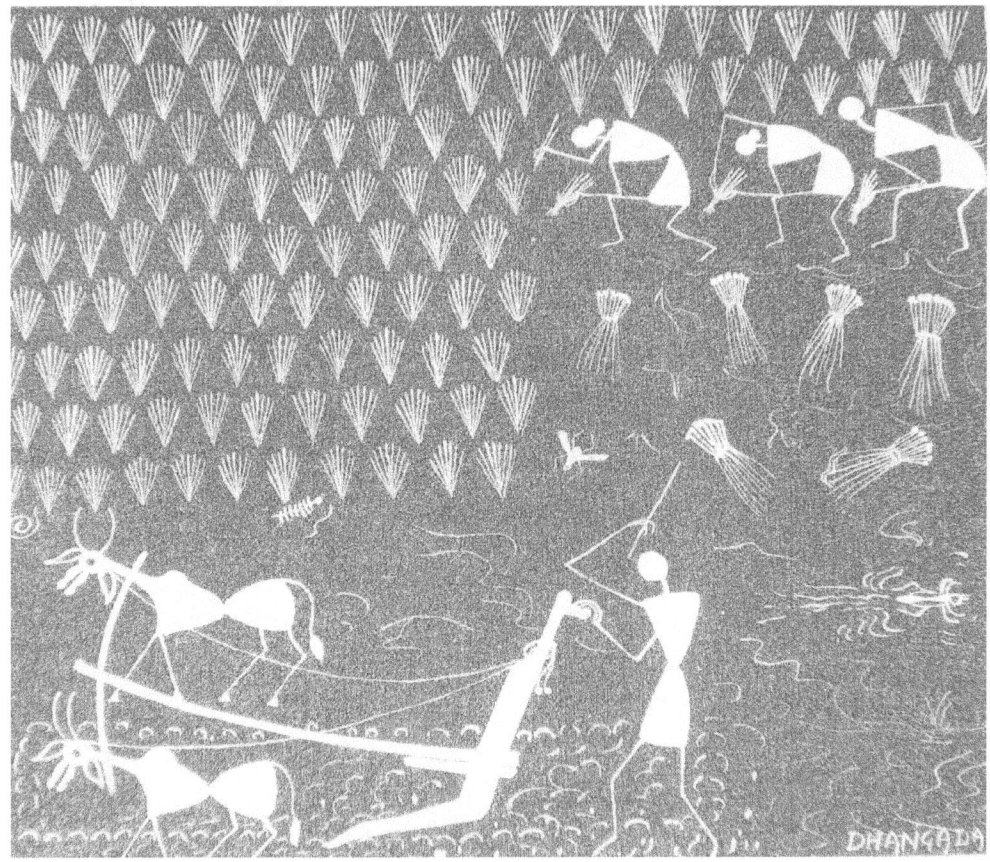

It takes 2-3 months to ripe the paddy fields and then the harvesting work begins...

Warli cuts this rice and dry it for a day in the Sun light and then tied up together to form a bundle.

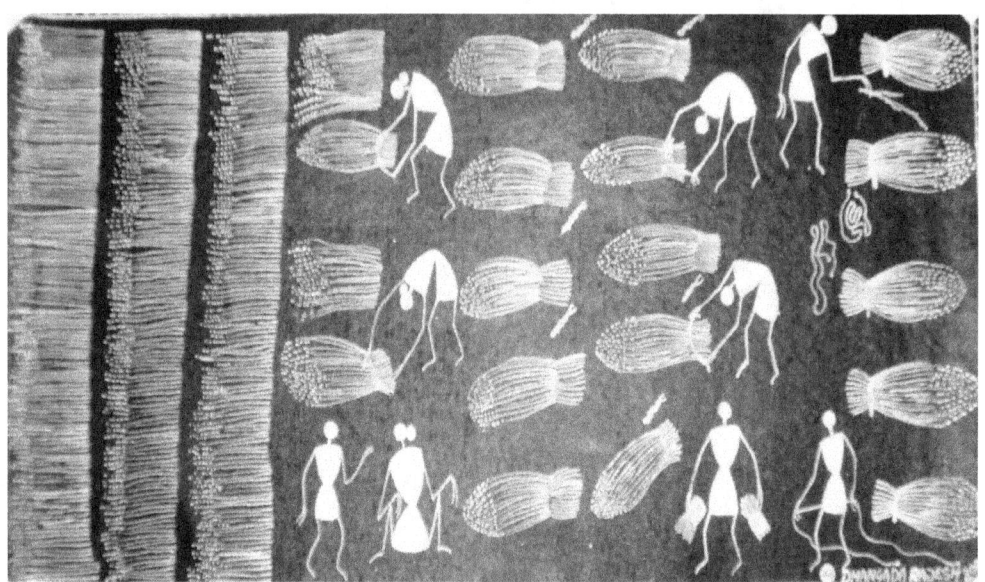

As the cultivated land is away from their homes; the bundle of rice need to be carried at thrashing ground near to home to thrash it and to protect from birds and cattle.

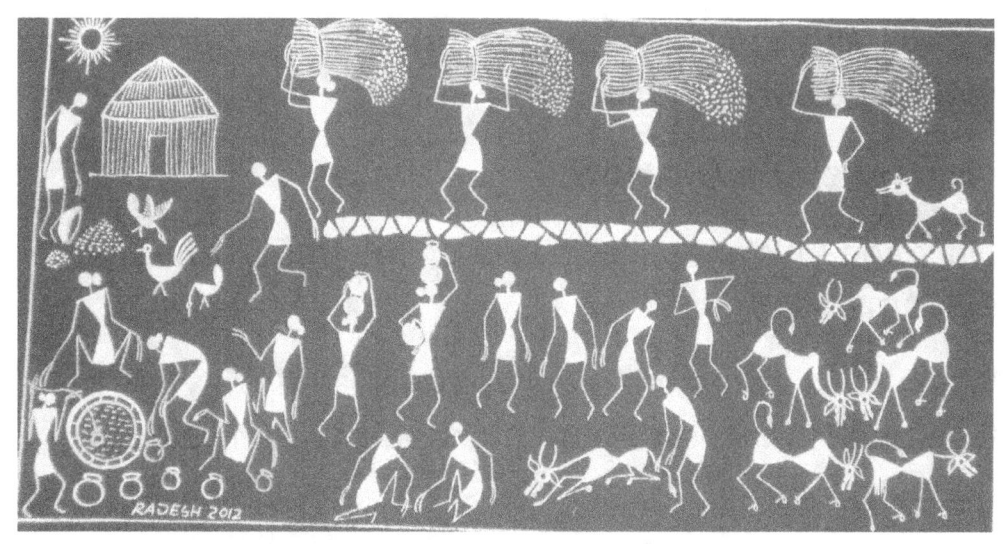

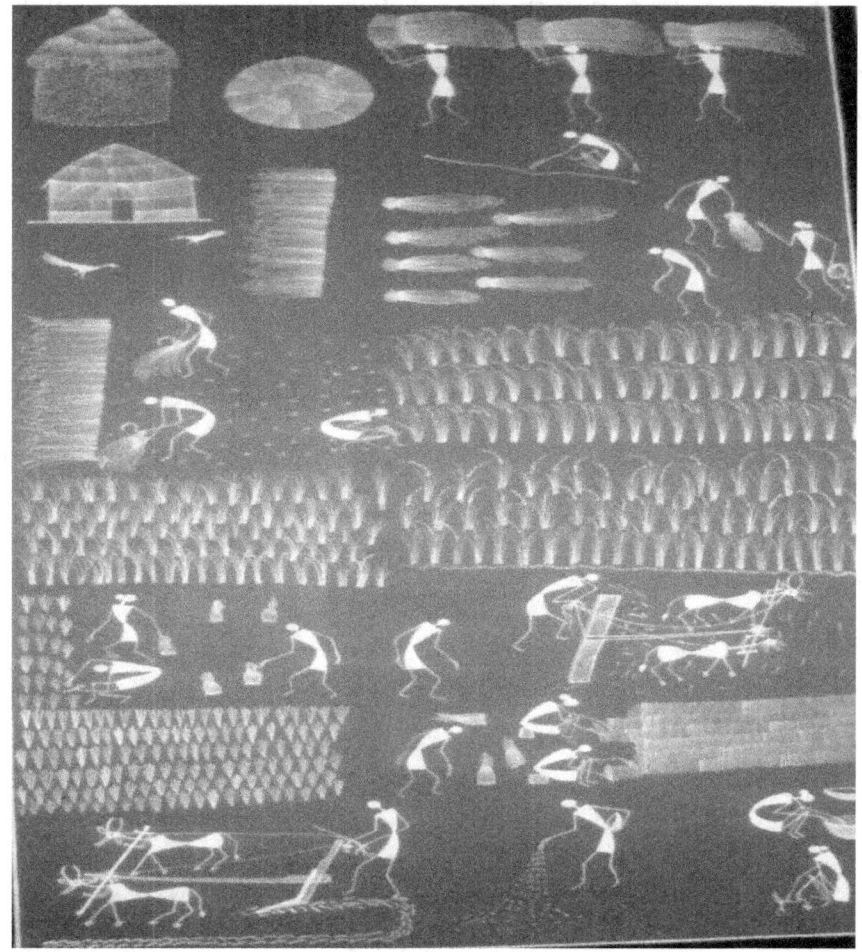

Here is the whole process of farming and harvesting in Warli painting.

Marriage Celebration

Marriage in Warli's life is one of the important sacred customs.

When the harvesting work is completed they become free and it is time to plan marriage of their elder boys and girls.

In Warli's culture marriage celebration begins with creation of pentagonal painting on wall called as Lagin (Marriage) chowk like this...

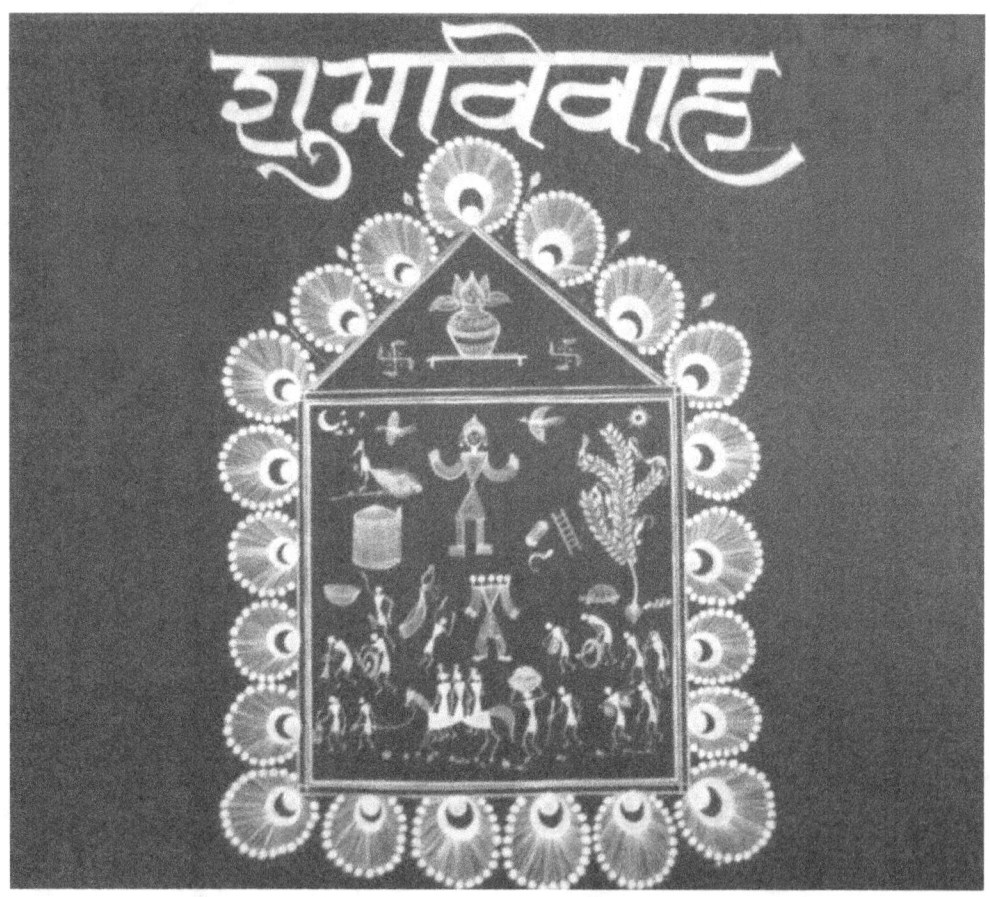

It is said that Warli painting is not drawn, it is written. Warli painting is just like literature.

This marriage chowk is the interpretation of Warli's deities. It is the holy custom of Warli people from the thousands of years old and they still obediently follow it.

It includes all the symbolic representation of the family deities, the sun, the moon and stars, bride and bridegroom sitting on the horse and their homeward procession with music players, monkeys on trees and other useful things.

Long ago, it was the rule that only married women can write the marriage chowk who knows all about the process and religious activities. Such women were specially invited to write this marriage chowk.

Some decade ago; Warli men also started to write this marriage chowk and now days most of the marriage chowks are written by men.

Here is one painting depicting about celebration of Warli's marriage function.

If you know their culture you can easily understand and can paint.

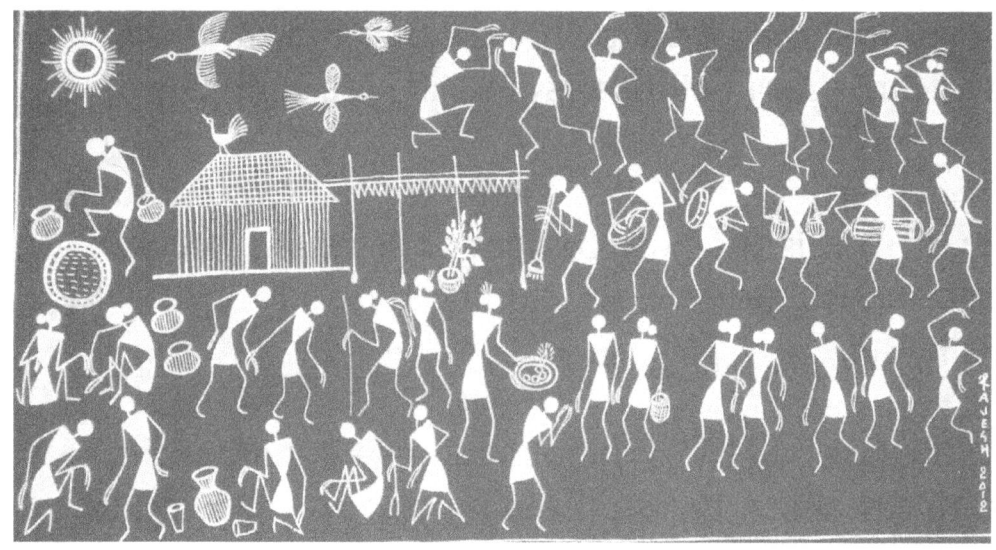

If you know the Warli's characters, you can do painting on any events of their cultural, social and spiritual work.

And you know this all at this point.

Let's see some more themes in Warli paintings...

Cowherd:

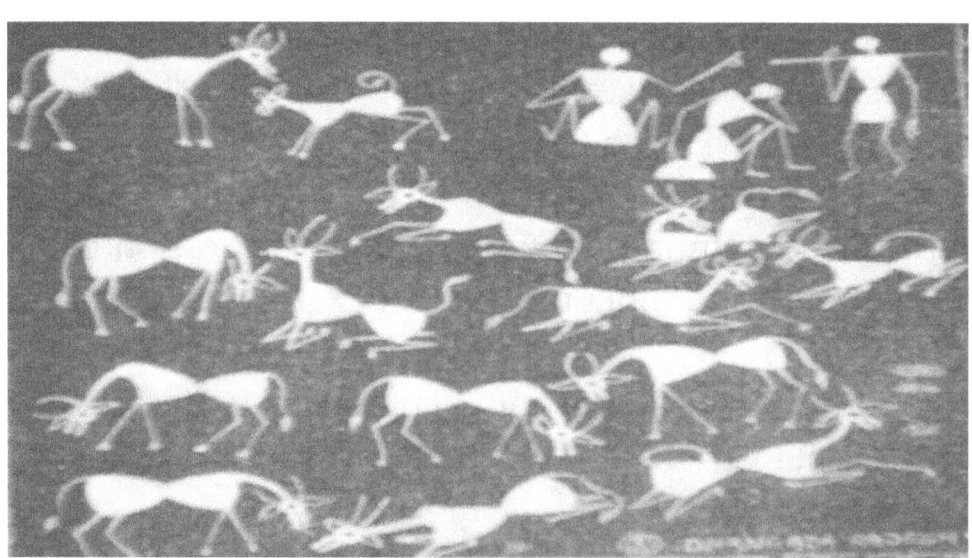

Worshiping:

Before starting any of the work Warli people worship for the nature to give them success in work taken. And again after successfully completion of their work Warli worship for thanks giving.

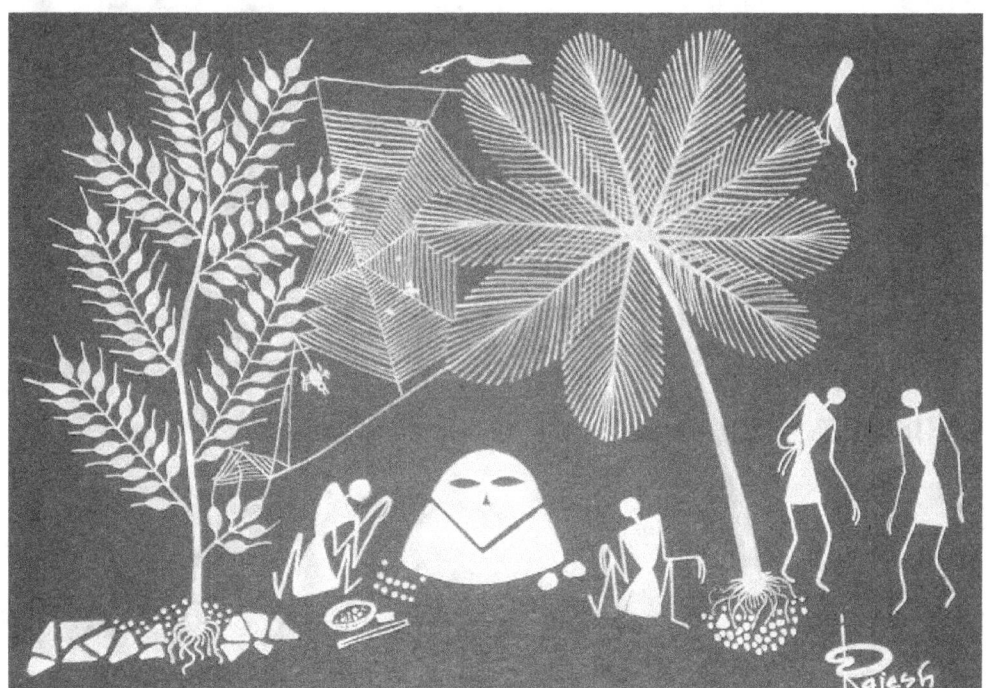

Hunting:

When Warli have free time or some festival reason they go out in the forest for hunting.

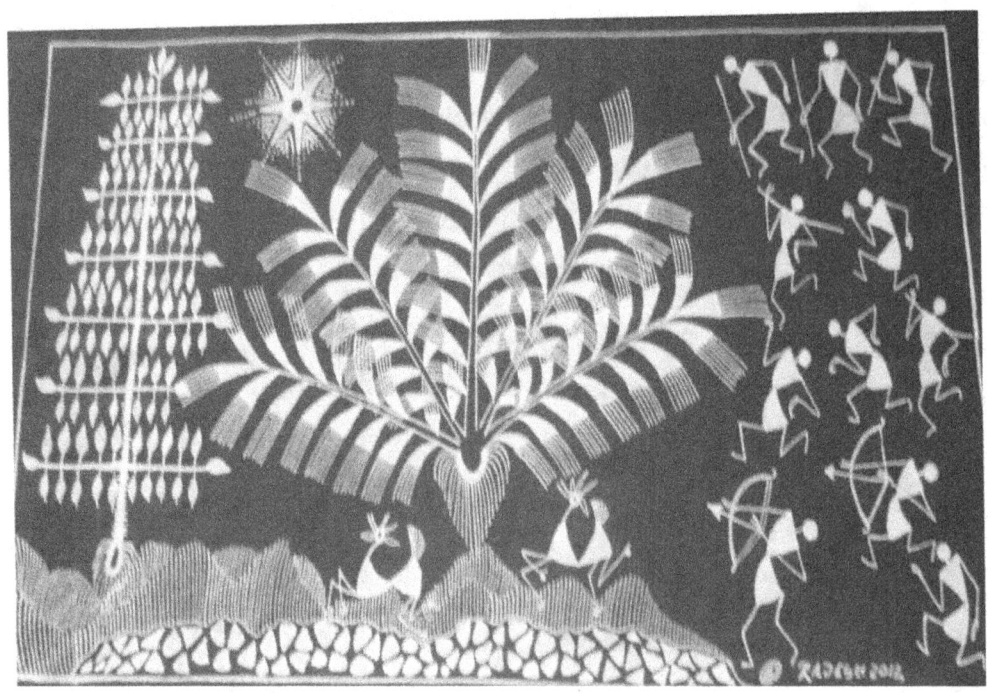

Selling Toddy Drink:

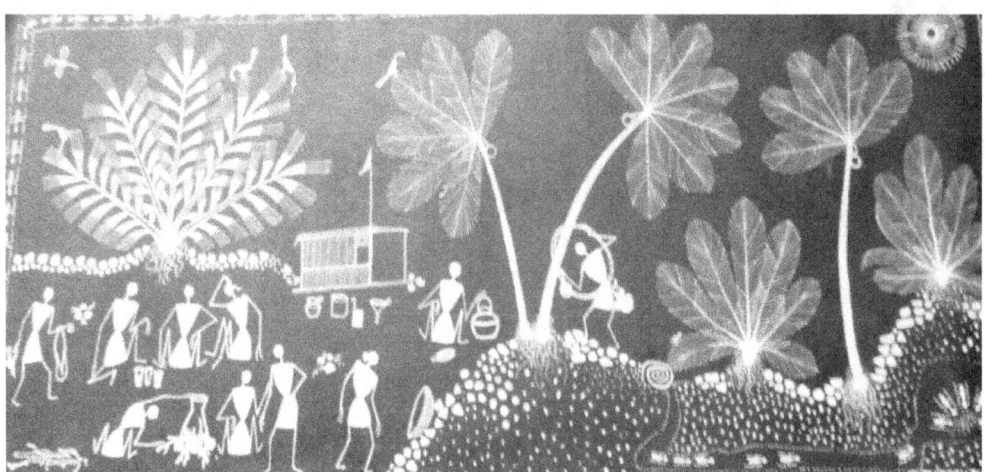

... And there are lots to draw. Now you have all the characters, you know how to draw them efficiently and you have some theme ready with you, right?

It's time to draw your FIRST Warli painting and my time to closing this book...

Thanking You!

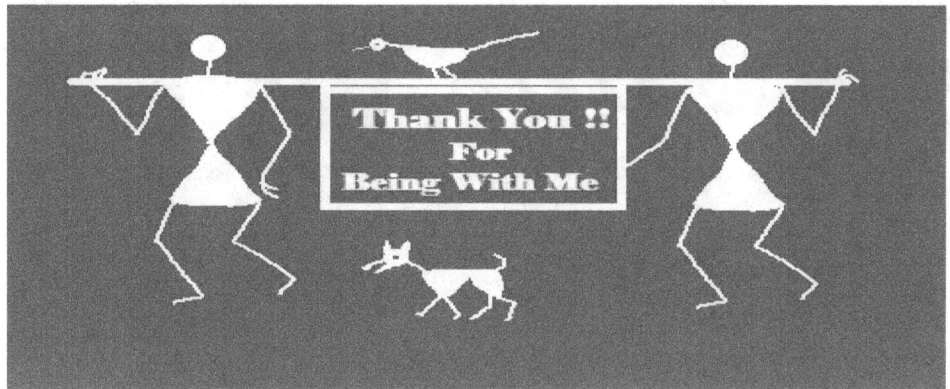

Thanks for being with me from start to the end. We have learned many characters and how to draw them for making your Warli painting amazing.

Also we have seen some of the themes commonly drawn in Warli paintings. And you are briefly introduced with various cultural and social activities of Warli community.

I will give you one practical... Download one of the Warli paintings from Internet and re-draw it with the Warli characters you have learned in this guide...and finally compare both. You will be glad to know that you are great.

So, make use of this book to learn yourself, create your own beautiful wall paintings and paint your pots, table lamps, flower-pots with Warli characters. And you can also teach to your child, make greeting-cards for your loved one, friends etc.

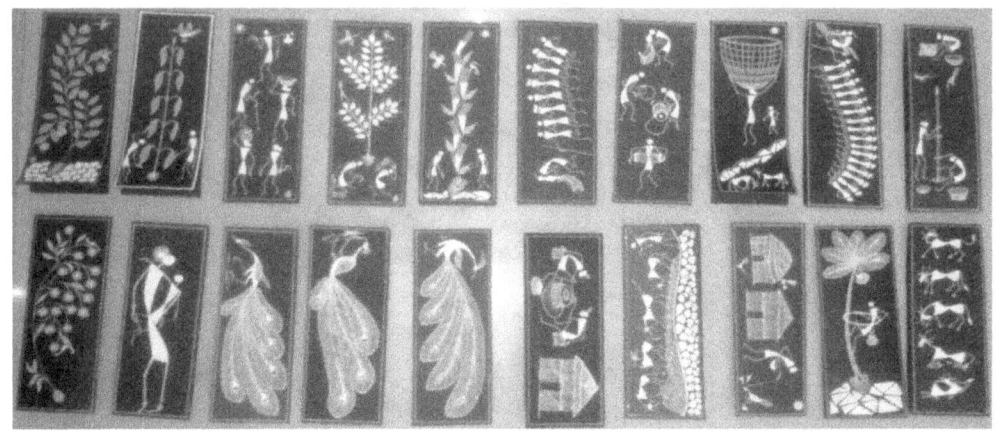

Decorate your home walls, shop or office...

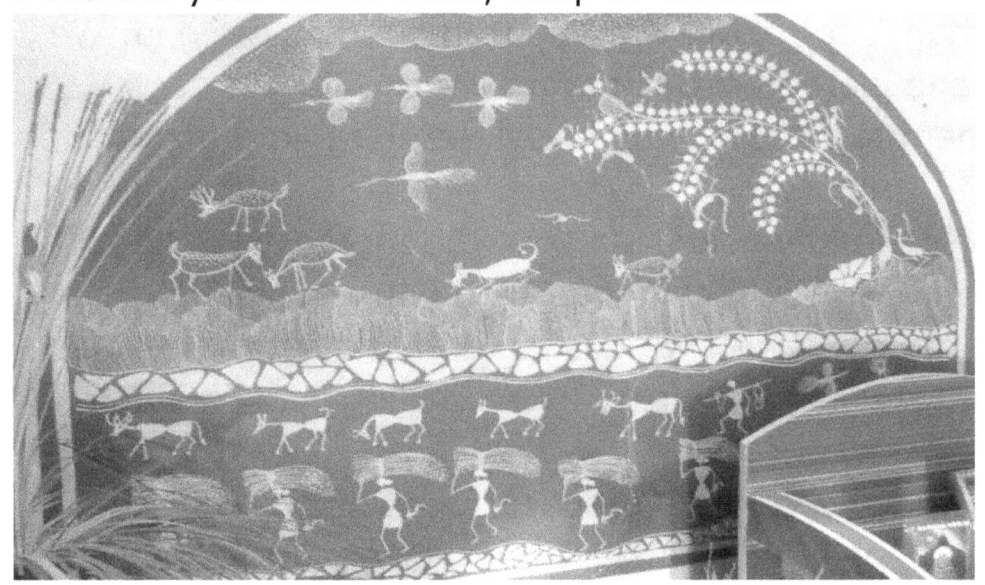

You can draw it at any place would like.

You can get lots of information about Warli and their culture over the internet but here is one website created by Aadivasi Yuva (Guys from Warli Community), where you can find more information about Warli culture, social life, real photos and videos and lots more... www.warli.adiyuva.in

I hope you found this book as informative and a guide for creating your own theme paintings.

Thanks once again for purchasing this book and spending some time with me.

Feel free to contact if help required and do share your work and feedback to me.

I am available at mrsantmali@gmail.com
Facebook: www.facebook.com/malisk82

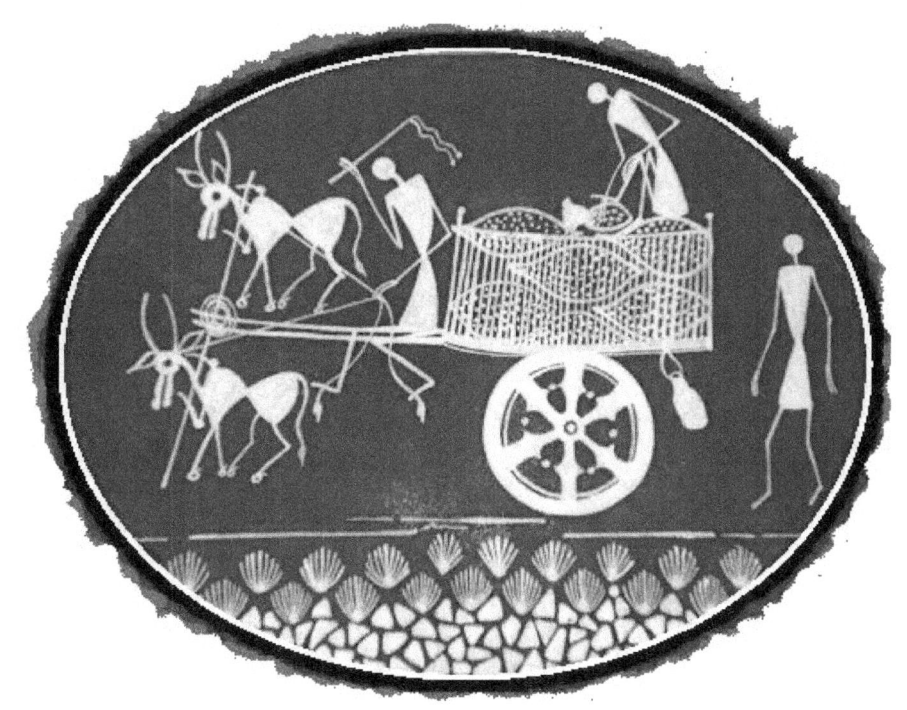

Santosh mali

www.ingramcontent.com/pod-product-compliance
Lightning Source LLC
Chambersburg PA
CBHW081314170526
45166CB00011B/3522